TO BE AN FBI
SPECIAL AGENT

Henry M. Holden

ZENITH PRESS

Dedication:
This book is dedicated to the men and women of the FBI.
May God bless you and keep you safe.

First published in 2005 by Zenith Press, an imprint of MBI Publishing Company, Galtier Plaza, Suite 200, 380 Jackson Street, St. Paul, MN 55101-3885 USA

Zenith Press titles are also available at discounts in bulk quantity for industrial or sales-promotional use. For details write to Special Sales Manager at MBI Publishing Company Wholesalers & Distributors, Galtier Plaza, Suite 200, 380 Jackson Street, St. Paul, MN 55101-3885 USA.

ISBN 0-7603-2118-3

On the title page: Traffic stops are an extremely dangerous part of an FBI special agent's job.

On the contents page: A statue at FBI Headquarters.

On the back cover: (upper right)The FBI works with other law enforcement agencies to permanently dismantle illegal drug operations. (bottom left) The Questioned Documents Unit in the labs examines and compares data on paper and other evidentiary materials. They have the ability to match torn or perforated edges of items such as paper, stamps, or matches. (upper left) Sacramento Emergency Response Team members are searching for two bodies believed to be buried under a concrete slab.

Author bio:
Henry M. Holden is the author of 12 adult books (including MBI Publishing Company's *To Be a U.S. Air Force Pilot*), 19 children's books, and more than 600 magazine articles on aviation history. In 1994 he received the New Jersey Institute of Technology's Author's Award, and that same year Holden was mentioned in the Congressional Record for his works on women in aviation. Holden has been an aviation commentator for the History Channel and lives in northwestern New Jersey.

Editorial: Steve Gansen and Lindsay Hitch
Design: Russell S. Kuepper

Printed in China

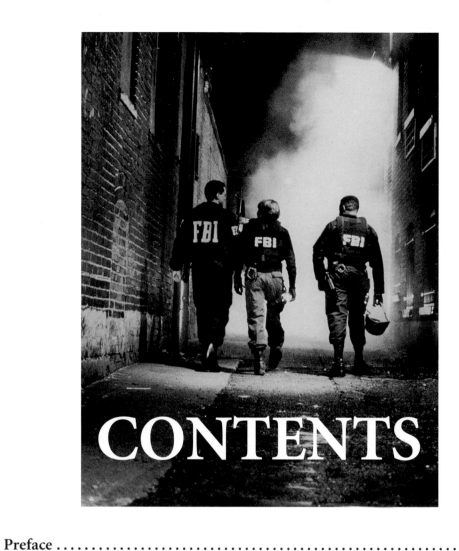

CONTENTS

Preface

The Federal Bureau of Investigation (FBI) is a symbol of America. Since its earliest days, the FBI has been involved in issues and controversies. Today, it is still in the crosshairs of history, however, now the issues are more complex as the world's borders become less defined. The FBI has taken a global approach to the war on terrorism. It must balance its mission against the rights of U.S. citizens. In an age when terrorists attempt to undermine and take advantage of the American rights to free speech, assembly, movement, self-incrimination, and due process, that is a challenge.

FBI Special Agents are trained to find the truth, document truth, and if necessary, present it to a judge and jury. Often, for security reasons, their work is never seen and goes unreported.

The FBI expects dedication and sacrifice from its personnel. One of its most valuable assets is its Special Agent cadre. But Special Agents could not do their challenging jobs without thousands of professional support personnel: electronics specialists, explosives experts, engineers, counterterrorism experts, laboratory analysts, and countless others. From the days of J. Edgar Hoover, the elimination of John Dillinger (Public Enemy No. 1) in the 1930s, the neutralization of the Ku Klux Klan, the major take-downs of organized crime families, and the safe return of hundreds of kidnapped victims, to their work after September 11, 2001, the FBI has succeeded many more times than it has failed.

In spite of innovative technology available to them, the FBI must still depend on the men and women who fill its ranks. They have made, and continue to make, personal sacrifices to protect America and prevent bad things from happening to its citizens. Every FBI employee I have met and spoke with has displayed a sense of personal integrity and sacrifice. One Special Agent in Charge (SAC) described it this way, "If you don't have credibility, you are not going to be effective."

The FBI has dealt with major events and public issues, which have given it a rich legacy and have been critical in shaping America's national security. Looking forward, the FBI's greatest challenges will be to carry on improving its intelligence capabilities and strengthening its information technology infrastructure. The FBI's international presence will continue to grow, and it will continue its tradition of excellence in carrying out its responsibilities overseas and in the United States.

"The FBI is about patriotism and public service," said one agent. "It is a job that transcends state borders; it is international in scope. We experience something different everyday—things that screenwriters write about." From my personal observations, patriotism is what fuels the engine of the FBI and that engine is in high gear. "You can't stop people bent on killing themselves in an act of terrorism, but you can try," said one Special Agent.

Special Agents will continue to train throughout their careers. Refresher training, such as this simulated raid, is important to keep the agents' skills sharp and perhaps save their lives.

New agent trainees practice various raid scenarios at Quantico.

Acknowledgments

Writing this book has been an immense pleasure and a learning experience. *To Be an FBI Special Agent* is the result of the FBI's willingness to open itself up to this writer. I was allowed access to its facilities in order to conduct interviews with senior management and current FBI Special Agents, and to observe and interview new agent trainees. This book would not have been possible, or as revealing, without the Bureau's full cooperation and trust that this would be an honest portrayal of the training that young men and women undergo to become FBI Special Agents. I have made every effort to keep that trust and to describe in detail the process of becoming an FBI Special Agent, while also respecting the security issues inherent in the process.

I spoke to many Special Agents who readily shared their backgrounds and experiences with me, even though they were overloaded with their own work. Public Affairs Specialist Kurt Crawford and Special Agents Angela Bell, Susan McKee, Steven Kodak, and Jim Margolin devoted a significant amount of time to me, from giving me tours to answering my hundreds of questions. I am also indebted to the following people: At the Newark field office, Special Agent (SA) Malinda Anderson, SA Bill Evanina, SA Sheri Evanina, and SAC Joseph Billy, Jr; At FBI Headquarters, Section Chief W. K. Williams, Supervising Special Agent (SSA) Ralph Thomas, Unit Chief SSA David Bowdich, SSA Brian Lamkin, SSA E. Reid Roe, Section Chief My Harrison, Assistant Director Cassandra M. Chandler, SSA Steve Anthony, and historian John Fox, Jr.; At the Strategic Information Operations Center, Michael Gabrini; In Quantico, Virginia, SSA Mike Quinn, Unit Chief Stephen Band, Ph.D., SSA Andy Bringuel, SSA Rand Bowling, SSA Andre Simons, SSA Tom Lintner, SSA Stan Letcher, SSA Lucy Hoover, SSA Bud Colonna, SSA Ken Myers, SSA Thomas Albright, SSA Butch Greathouse, SSA Kate Killham, and SSA Tim Donavan; At the FBI laboratories in Quantico, SSA Ann Todd, SSA Dayna Better; and SSA Marshall Stone in Springfield, Missouri.

Space limitations bar me from including everyone's valuable insights.

Thanks to Steve Gansen, my editor, who went to bat for me and sold my idea for this book to MBI Publishing Company, and for his continued friendship and professionalism.

Of course, my special thanks go to my best friend and wife Nancy, who has always been understanding and supportive of the need I have for, and enjoyment I get from, writing. To everyone, my thanks; if I have forgotten anyone, please forgive me and know that I am grateful.

Henry M. Holden

Shotgun training is a part of every agent's training. All agents must qualify and maintain their qualification over the course of their career.

ONE

Sixty years ago, FBI physical and defensive training was conducted on the rooftop of the Department of Justice.

Application

This 1940s FBI Special Agent is using an early portable telephone link—an ancient forerunner to today's palm-sized cellular phone.

The agency now known as the Federal Bureau of Investigation (FBI) was founded in 1908, when U.S. Attorney General Charles J. Bonaparte appointed an unnamed group of Special Agents to be the investigative force of the Department of Justice. The Special Agent force became the Bureau of Investigation in 1909, and following a series of name changes, the FBI received its present title in 1935.

The FBI originally had one responsibility: to ensure domestic tranquility by protecting the American people from domestic and foreign enemies, while honoring and defending the Constitution of the United States of America. From that somewhat vague description of responsibility, the FBI has grown to a force of more than 12,000 Special Agents and over 16,000 professional support personnel. No other law enforcement agency has the FBI's resources, reputation, prestige, and global presence. Today, the FBI is charged with enforcing more than 360 federal statutes, and among some of its grave responsibilities are the investigation of terrorist activities, violent crimes, drug trafficking, espionage, civil rights violations, and white-collar crimes.

Each symbol and color in the FBI seal has special significance. The dominant blue field of the seal and the scales on the shield represent justice. The endless circle of 13 stars denotes unity of purpose as exemplified by the original 13 states. The laurel leaf symbolizes academic honors, distinction, and fame, as it has since early civilization. There are exactly 46 leaves on the two branches, since there were 46 states in the union when the FBI was founded in 1908. The significance of the red and white parallel stripes lies in their colors. Red traditionally stands for courage, valor, and strength, while white conveys cleanliness, light, truth, and peace. As in the American flag, the red bars exceed the white by one. The motto, "Fidelity, Bravery, Integrity," succinctly describes the motivating force behind the men and women of the FBI. The peaked beveled edge, which circumscribes the seal, symbolizes the severe challenges confronting the FBI and the ruggedness of the organization. The gold color in the seal conveys its overall value.

On July 26, 1908, Attorney General Charles Bonaparte ordered nine newly hired detectives, 13 civil rights investigators, and 12 accountants to take on investigative assignments, including antitrust, peonage, and land fraud. He wrote to President Theodore Roosevelt that he was determined "to establish a force of well-educated investigators of good character, subject to extremely strict discipline and supervision."

EVOLUTION OF THE FEDERAL BUREAU OF INVESTIGATION

July 26, 1908—No specific name assigned; referred to as Special Agent Force
March 16, 1909—Bureau of Investigation
July 1, 1932—U.S. Bureau of Investigation
August 10, 1933—Division of Investigation (the division also included the Bureau of Prohibition)
July 1, 1935—Federal Bureau of Investigation

FBI MISSION

The mission of the FBI is to protect and defend the United States against terrorist and foreign intelligence threats, to uphold and enforce the criminal laws of the United States, and to provide leadership and criminal justice services to federal, state, municipal, and international agencies and partners.

FBI CORE VALUES

The FBI will strive for excellence in all aspects of its missions. In pursuing these missions, the FBI and its employees will be true to, and exemplify, the following core values:

1. Adherence to the rule of law and the rights conferred to all under the U.S. Constitution;

2. Integrity through everyday ethical behavior;

3. Accountability by accepting responsibility for their actions and decisions and the consequences of their actions and decisions;

4. Fairness in dealing with people; and

5. Leadership through example, both at work and in their communities.

On July 22, 1934, John Dillinger, America's "Public Enemy Number 1," walked into the Biograph Theater in Chicago. From September 1933 to July 1934, Dillinger had robbed 10 banks, killed 10 men, wounded seven others, robbed a police arsenal, and staged three jailbreaks. As Dillinger left the theater, he sensed something was wrong and reached to his right front pocket for a pistol. Agents fired. Dillinger fell, mumbled a few words, and died. The successful conclusion to the Dillinger manhunt was the beginning of the end of the gangster era and a cornerstone in the evolution of the Bureau.

During the early and mid-1930s several crucial decisions solidified the position of the BOI, the forerunner of the FBI, as the nation's leading law enforcement agency. Responding to the high-profile kidnapping of Charles Lindbergh's baby, Congress passed a federal kidnapping statute on June 22, 1932. In the wake of the Kansas City massacre, where federal agents were gunned down, Congress passed what became known as the May/June (1934) Crime Bills, which made it a federal crime to kill or assault a federal officer. Congress also created the Fugitive Felon Act, gave the BOI full powers of arrest in crimes under its jurisdiction (prior to this a United States marshal had to be called to make an arrest), and authorized BOI agents to carry firearms. *Henry M. Holden*

PROFESSIONAL SUPPORT EMPLOYEES

The majority of the FBI's workforce is made up of professional support employees who work alongside and in support of the Special Agents. Some professional support positions only require the applicant be 16 years old and possess a high school diploma or GED; many others require college degrees, or even advanced degrees, and specific work experience. All professional support personnel must complete the same application and go through the same background investigation process as a Special Agent does.

In September 1933, gangster "Machine Gun" Kelly reputedly coined the nickname "g-men." The legend that Kelly shouted, "Don't shoot, g-man, don't shoot," while he was being arrested is doubtful. "G-man," short for government man, quickly became synonymous with FBI Special Agents in the public's imagination.

WOMEN IN THE FBI

Women have always played a pivotal role in the daily operations of the FBI. In the 1920s, three female Special Agents were hired for the Bureau of Investigation (later renamed the Federal Bureau of Investigation): Mrs. Alaska P. Davidson, October 1922; Mrs. Jessie B. Duckstein, November 1923; and Miss Lenore Houston, November 1924. In May 1924, Director J. Edgar Hoover requested the resignations of Mrs. Duckstein and Mrs. Davidson during a force reduction. On November 1928, Miss Houston resigned from the Bureau of Investigation and was the last woman to serve in the Special Agent position for 44 years. Today, women serve as executive managers, oversee FBI field offices, legal attaché offices, and manage large divisions at FBI Headquarters.

QUALIFICATIONS
FOR THE SPECIAL AGENT POSITION

To qualify for training as an FBI Special Agent, an individual must be a U.S. citizen and between 23 and 37 years of age at the time of appointment. The maximum age of 37 at the time of appointment ensures that Special Agents will be able to complete 20 years of service by the age of 57, which is the mandatory retirement age. Special Agents must serve for at least 20 years to qualify for retirement. The average age of new agents is 30, and the applicants usually have a background of significant work experience, discipline, and maturity.

"The critical skills the FBI is looking for change with the needs of the Bureau," said one agent. "My advice to someone thinking of becoming an FBI Special Agent is to stay away from all drugs—period. Do well in school, take a major you like because you are likely to do well in it, have a clean driving record, no criminal record, and if

> Federal law requires that Special Agents retire by age 57. In rare circumstances, the FBI director may grant one-year extensions, up to age 60, for particular Special Agents.

J. Edgar Hoover became the director of the FBI in 1924 and held the post for 48 years. In January 1928, he established a formal training course for new agents and insisted that all agents wear ties and jackets and set a good example in their communities. Today, the director of the FBI is appointed by the president and confirmed by the Senate. In October 1976, Congress passed Public Law 94-503, which limits the term of each FBI director to 10 years.

Director William H. Webster (1977–1987) placed emphasis on investigative "quality" cases by focusing the Bureau's efforts on three priority programs: white-collar crime, organized crime, and foreign counterintelligence. Later, illegal drugs, counterterrorism, and violent crimes also became priority programs. The concentration of resources on these programs brought great success against Soviet and East Bloc intelligence, as more than 40 spies were arrested between 1977 and 1985.

not in excellent physical condition, start getting in shape long before you fill out the application. You will be physically challenged, to be sure."

Applicants must possess a four-year degree from an accredited college or university and have a minimum of three years of fulltime employment. They must also possess a valid driver's license and pass a polygraph examination, an extensive background check, a drug test, and a color vision test. Vision requirements are that uncorrected vision cannot be worse than 20/200 (by the Snellen standard) uncorrected, and when corrected to 20/20 in one eye, it cannot be not worse than 20/40 in the other eye. These corrective eye surgeries—laser-assisted *in situ* keratomileusis (Lasik), automated lamellar keratoplasty (ALK), radial keratotomy (RK), and photorefractive keratectomy (PRK)—are acceptable procedures for Special Agent applicants. However, the FBI will retest applicants who have had Lasik surgery 90 days after the procedure and those who have had all other eye surgeries one year afterwards.

This photo from the 1930s shows Special Agents being trained to search for fingerprints.

Training at Quantico's pistol range in the 1970s.

Michael Alfonso
UFAP - Murder,
Aggravated Stalking

Usama Bin Laden
Murder of U.S. Nationals
Outside the United States;
Conspiracy to Murder U.S.
Nationals Outside the
United States; Attack on
a Federal Facility Resulting in Death

James J. Bulger
RICO - Murder,
Conspiracy to Commit Murder;
Conspiracy to Commit Extortion,
Narcotics Distribution,
Conspiracy to Commit Money Laundering;
Extortion; Money Laundering

Genero Espinosa Dorantes
UFAP - Criminal Homicide

Robert William Fisher
UFAP - First Degree Murder,
Arson of an Occupied Structure

Victor Manuel Gerena
Bank Robbery;
UFAP - Armed Robbery;
Theft From Interstate
Shipment

Glen Stewart Godwin
UFAP - Murder, Escape

Richard Steve Goldberg
Sexual Exploitation of Children
(Production of Child Pornography);
UFAP - Lewd Acts Upon a Child,
Possession of Child Pornography

Diego Leon Montoya Sanchez
Conspiracy to Import and Possess
With Intent to Deliver Cocaine;
Possession With Intent to Deliver Cocaine;
Money Laundering; RICO - Drug Trafficking;
Conspiracy to Distribute or Manufacture
Cocaine Abroad With Knowledge or
Intent That it be Imported into the United States

Donald Eugene Webb
UFAP - Murder; Attempted Burglary

the FBI's **ten most wanted** *fugitives*

EIGHT GERMAN SABOTEURS

GEORGE JOHN DASCH

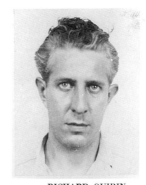
ERNEST PETER BURGER

RICHARD QUIRIN

HEINRICH HARM HEINCK

EDWARD KERLING

HERBERT HANS HAUPT

WERNER THIEL

HERMANN OTTO NEUBAUER

In June 1942, a major, yet unsuccessful, attempt at sabotage was made on American soil. Two German submarines let off four saboteurs each at Amagansett, Long Island, New York, and Ponte Vedra Beach, Florida. The men had been trained in explosives, chemistry, secret writing, and how to blend into American surroundings. While still in German clothes, the New York group encountered a coast guard sentinel patrolling the beach who ultimately allowed them to pass. However, afraid of capture, saboteur George Dasch turned himself in and assisted the FBI in locating and arresting the rest of the team. The swift capture of these Nazi saboteurs helped to allay fear of Axis subversion and bolster Americans' faith in the FBI.

Left: The FBI's "10 most-wanted fugitives" list was created on March 14, 1950, when a reporter asked the Bureau for the names and descriptions of the "toughest guys" the Bureau would like to capture. The resulting story generated so much publicity and had so much appeal that Hoover implemented the "10 most-wanted fugitives" program. To date, 478 fugitives have been on the list; 449 of them have been apprehended or located, and of those, 146 fugitives have been captured or located because of citizen cooperation.

After the attacks on September 11, 2001, the FBI identified several critical skills that the Bureau still needed. These include computer science, engineering, foreign counterintelligence, military intelligence, physical sciences, and foreign language skills in Arabic, Farsi, Pashtu, Urdu, Chinese, Japanese, Korean, Russian, Spanish, and Vietnamese.

STEPS IN THE FBI SPECIAL AGENT APPLICATION PROCESS

There are three major steps in the selection process of an FBI Special Agent. They are the completion of the application checklist for the special agent position, the short form application titled "preliminary application for special agent position," in which personal information, including name, address, highest level of education, any drug use, and brief employment history, is used to determine qualifications, suitability, and availability, and the special agent qualifications questionnaire (SAQQ).

The application checklist for the special agent position is a series of 49 statements outlining the minimum prerequisites for the position, and applicants must acknowledge in writing that they are willing and able to meet them. Examples of what is listed in the application checklist are the ability to engage in strenuous and potentially dangerous duties, and to routinely carry firearms (and use them if necessary) in a variety of life-threatening situations. All of the functions listed pertain to requirements considered necessary for the effective performance of the Special Agent. If applicants meet these requirements, and if the information on the SAQQ indicates the applicants are competitive for FBI testing, then the applicant coordinator will advise them to report to a local FBI field office for phase I testing.

In the wake of Director Hoover's death in May 1972, Director Clarence M. Kelley (1973–1977) refocused FBI investigative priorities by placing less emphasis on the quantity of cases and focusing more on the quality of cases handled. He was instrumental in establishing a set of investigative guidelines to address the concerns of Bureau critics and give the FBI the confidence of having public and legal authority behind its use of irreplaceable investigative techniques like wiretaps, informants, and undercover agents.

The special agent qualifications questionnaire (SAQQ) is used to determine the competitiveness of each applicant with the following factors taken into consideration:

· Investigative needs of the FBI

· Academic qualifications

· Professional certifications/licenses (e.g. CPA, Bar)

· Direct supervisory experience

· Previous law enforcement/federal government/military experience

· Professional work experience

· Awards, professional recognition, medals, etc.

· Successful completion of the FBI Honors Internship Program

· Community service/volunteer work

· Veterans' preference (a one-time preference)

Once hired, all FBI employees must maintain their eligibility for top-secret security clearance, undergo a limited background check every five years, and submit to random drug tests throughout their careers. It costs about $9,775 to hire an agent.

In 1940, a small plane carrying 25 people, including two FBI employees, crashed in a cornfield in Virginia, killing all on board. FBI representatives went to the crash site to claim FBI property and offered its fingerprinting expertise to positively identify eight of the 25 victims. The crash demonstrated a need for a national disaster squad, which would have experts ready to travel to the scene of a disaster at a moment's notice to assist local authorities in identifying victims. To date, the FBI disaster squad has assisted in 207 disasters involving some 8,235 victims. It has identified 4,490 victims by fingerprints, palm prints, or footprints. During the 1990s, this elite group of experts was involved in many high-profile incidents, in the United States and abroad, including Operation Desert Storm; the storming of the Branch Davidian complex in Waco, Texas; the bombings of the Oklahoma City federal building and Khobar Towers in Saudi Arabia; and the crashes of Trans-world Airlines Flight 800, ValuJet Flight 592, and EgyptAir Flight 990.

On May 12, 1972, L. Patrick Gray III, acting director of the FBI, announced that women could apply for the special agent position. Two months later, Ms. Susan Lynn Roley and Ms. Joanne E. Pierce became Special Agents of the modern FBI. Their acceptance into the new agent training class opened doors for women interested in becoming FBI Special Agents.

Of 12,221 Special Agents, more than 18 percent are women. Among the 16,613 FBI support employees, more than 65 percent are women.

FBI SPECIAL AGENT STATISTICS (AS OF SEPTEMBER 30, 2004)

American Indian	49
Asian	436
Black	660
Hispanic	920
White	10,226
TOTALS	**12,291**
All Females	2,278

On November 24, 1932, the Bureau of Investigation (BOI) established a technical laboratory in the Southern Railway Building on 13th Street and Pennsylvania Avenue NW, Washington, D.C. It provided services to other federal, state, local, and even foreign law enforcement agencies.

PHASE I TEST PREPARATION

Applicants must bring a driver's license to phase I and phase II testing. If the license does not have a photo, they must provide an additional form of photo identification. During the process, the applicants will be fingerprinted.

The applicants must not bring any of the following items to either phase I or phase II testing: the *FBI Special Agent Selection Process: Applicant Information Booklet*; reading or reference materials such as newspapers, dictionaries, and textbooks; pens or pencils (these will be provided); work-related materials; briefcases; papers, such as notification letters, notes, resumes, and blank paper; beepers or pagers; cellular phones; and tape recorders, cassettes, compact disc players, radios, calculators, or cameras. Alarms on wrist watches must be turned off. No firearms are allowed. Those in law enforcement positions will not be permitted to bring firearms into any FBI space or the testing facility.

PHASE I TESTING

Before the written test, and again later during the application process, the applicants will see a film that stresses both the significance of the special agent position as well as the potential dangers that an armed agent might face. At any time the applicants may remove themselves from the selection process if they feel they cannot carry out the duties of an FBI Special Agent.

For the first test, the FBI recommends wearing comfortable clothes that would be appropriate in an office environment. The first phase of the testing process consists of a battery of three pencil and paper tests: biodata inventory, cognitive ability test, and situational judgment test. Some agents have compared these tests to the graduate management admission test (GMAT) or law school admissions test (LSAT) "on steroids."

The biodata inventory contains 47 questions and measures applicants' ability to organize, plan, and prioritize; to maintain a positive image; to evaluate information; and to make judgment decisions. It also measures initiative, motivation, the ability to adapt to changing situations, and more.

For the biodata inventory, it is important that the applicants' self-descriptions are honest and accurate. Doing otherwise will distort the test score and negatively affect their performance.

A sample question may be:

In connection with your work, in which of the following have you taken the most pride?
A. Having been able to avoid any major controversies.
B. Having gotten where you are on your own.
C. Having been able to work smoothly with people.
D. Having provided a lot of new ideas, good or bad.
E. Having been able to do well whatever management has requested.

In this example, applicants select the answer that best describes what they honestly take pride in with regard to their personal work ethic. Applicants have 45 minutes to complete this inventory.

The cognitive ability test consists of three parts. Applicants must work quickly and accurately to complete as many items as possible. This is the only test for which applicants can prepare. There are math test preparation guides available in bookstores and libraries and, in addition, examples of the cognitive ability test items can be found in the *Special Agent Exam Preparation Manual* available from the special agent recruiter.

This test will measure the applicants' knowledge of algebra, geometry, and applied arithmetic, such as percentages, ratios, and averages. The first part of this test measures mathematical reasoning. Applicants have 29 minutes to answer 25 questions. The second part measures the ability to interpret data from tables and graphs, and applicants have 24 minutes to answer 25 questions. The third part of the test measures the ability to use learned mathematical relationships and reasoning, skills in data analysis and interpretation, and more. The applicant has 22 minutes to answer 25 questions.

The situational judgment test is a common-sense test that has 33 descriptions of problem situations. For each problem there are several alternative actions that can be taken to deal with it. The applicants must make two judgments for each problem—the most likely and the least likely.

Here is an example:

You are shopping when you notice a man robbing a store at gunpoint. What would you do?
A. Leave the store as quickly as possible and call the police.
B. Try to apprehend the robber yourself.
C. Follow the man and call the police as soon as he appears settled somewhere.
D. Nothing, as you do not wish to get involved in the matter.

The passing score for phase I testing is based on the combination of all three tests rather than the individual scores of each test. The biodata inventory equals 40 percent, the situational judgment test is another 40 percent, and the cognitive ability test is worth 20 percent.

After taking these tests, applicants will sign a nondisclosure statement and receive written notification stating pass or fail status within 30 days. A passing grade means applicants must submit the 15-page application for employment (FD-140 form) within 10 days. The completed FD-140 will be reviewed, and the applicants' qualifications will be assessed again to determine their competitiveness. Not all applicants who pass phase I will be granted an interview. Only those candidates deemed the "most competitive" will proceed to phase II. One issue that will weigh in the competitiveness factor is the individuals' past work records of sick days, personal days taken, and vacation days. The applicants who receive a failing grade may be eligible for a one-time retest one year later.

For those candidates who are married or engaged, later in the application process the FBI will interview the spouses or fiancés separately and advise them of the FBI policy regarding pay, relocation, round-the-clock availability, firearms in the home, potential danger inherent in the job, and travel. The FBI will also inform the spouses or fiancés that because of the intense physical and academic schedule, there will be limited access to the candidates while in training. "My fiancé broke off our engagement after that interview, and I was upset for a while," said one agent. "But looking back it was a good thing because he would not have been able to stay married to an FBI agent."

Applicants who pass both phase I and phase II testing are given a conditional appointment as a Special Agent, contingent on successful completion of a background investigation, security clearance, pre-employment polygraph, physical examination, and drug testing.

Part of the application process is signing a release where the applicants must also provide their social security number. The signed release allows any Special Agent to obtain any information pertaining to the applicants' certified public accountant (CPA) or state bar records, as well as any grievance records, employment, military, and educational records—including, but not limited to, academic, achievement, attendance, athletic, personal history, and disciplinary records. The release also allows any Special Agent to access the applicants' medical records; credit records, including credit card and payment device numbers; and law enforcement records, including, but not limited to, any record of charge, prosecution or conviction for criminal or civil offenses, and driving record.

During the process a Special Agent asks applicants why specifically do they want to join the FBI and if they understand the inherent dangers and hardships of the job. To give the applicants all the information necessary to make an informed decision, a Special Agent will tell, in detail, the hardships of the job, including the wedding anniversaries, holidays, and birthdays they will miss. A Special Agent is considered on duty 24 hours a day, seven days a week, and because of this requirement FBI Special Agents are not allowed supplemental employment or income. (Passive income, such as that gained from investments in stocks, bonds, and real estate, is excluded.) They may be transferred at any time, to any field office, based on the needs of the Bureau. In addition, they will probably have to serve temporary duty (TDY) in another city, and possibly overseas, sometimes for extended periods.

The applicants must provide a State Department form 240 for themselves or any of their relatives who were born outside of the United States. If the candidate is a naturalized citizen, he or she must provide a naturalization certificate number. The applicants must also list the last place of residence and year of death for any of their deceased relatives. If applicants have been married more than once, they must list all former spouses. It is critical to the applicants' potential career as an FBI Special Agent that the information on this form be accurate and truthful. It will be used later in the polygraph examination and the background check.

PHASE II TESTING AND INTERVIEW

Before the interview begins, the following directions are read to the applicant:

"We'd like to spend the next hour getting to know more about you. During the interview, we will ask you to tell us how you've dealt with various kinds of situations in the past. In answering our questions, you can draw on experiences in family, work, school, or social situations and how you handled them. We would like you to describe the situation, tell us what you did in that situation and how things turned out.

"We will be asking you 15 questions. Feel free to take a few moments to think about the answer you would like to give for each question. If you would like a question repeated, please ask. You'll be doing most of the talking during the interview. We will be taking notes while you talk, to document the interview.

"Remember, be as specific and detailed as possible in describing the situation, your actions, and the outcome of your actions."

FBI Special Agents who serve as assessors will evaluate these tests, for they have been trained on how to rate the applicants' performance during their interviews by using standardized scoring criteria. The evaluators receive no application or background information on the applicants and, therefore, know nothing about them at the time of the interview.

The evaluators are trained to keep each interview moving and have each completed within 60 minutes. The applicants must remember to keep all answers concise. Long-winded answers will detract from their ability to complete the interview.

There is one passing score based on the combined outcome of the interview and the written exercise rather than individual passing scores for each test. The interview is weighted three times more than the written

Special Agents enter as General Schedule (GS) 10 grade level employees and can advance to the GS-13 grade level in field non-supervisory assignments. All Special Agents may qualify for availability pay, which is an additional premium compensation for unscheduled duty equaling 25 percent of the agent's base salary. Special Agents work a minimum of 50 hours a week, often 70–90 hours a week.

In the phase II test, the one-hour 30-minute written exercise will require the applicants to write a detailed report to the editor of a newspaper. This is designed to measure the applicants' ability to attend to details, communicate in writing, evaluate, and make judgment decisions.

"I grew up on Erle Stanley Gardner novels, and I enjoyed reading about the investigative work," said Section Chief of the Organized Crime Section W. K. Williams. "I knew I wanted to go into law enforcement, and the FBI had the reputation of being the premier law enforcement agency, so I decided [it was] my choice. I remember the murder of the three civil rights workers [in Mississippi in June 1964]. That was a significant event in my life, and it made me more determined to become an FBI Special Agent."

FBI Badge.

HONORS INTERNSHIP

Each summer, the FBI selects outstanding undergraduate juniors and graduate students to participate in the FBI Honors Internship Program in Washington, D.C. Due to the very selective and highly competitive nature of the honors internship program, a limited number of internships are awarded each summer to students with at least a 3.0 grade point average. The FBI will only select those individuals who possess strong academic credentials, outstanding character, a high degree of motivation, and the willingness to represent the FBI upon returning to their respective campuses. In order to be considered, individuals must interview on a competitive level. Finalists must undergo an extensive background investigation and drug-screening test. The director of the FBI makes the final approval decision.

The FBI Headquarters in Washington, D.C., opened shortly after Director Hoover died in 1972.

THE MOST EFFECTIVE WEAPON AGAINST CRIME IS COOPERATION... THE EFFORTS OF ALL LAW ENFORCEMENT AGENCIES WITH THE SUPPORT AND UNDERSTANDING OF THE AMERICAN PEOPLE.

FIDELITY BRAVERY INTEGRITY

The courtyard of the J. Edgar Hoover FBI Building in Washington, D.C., carries a quote by Hoover: "The most effective weapon against crime is cooperation. The efforts of all law enforcement agencies with the support and understanding of the American people."

Statue at FBI Headquarters.

The second phase of the testing process consists of a one-hour structured interview and a written exercise. The 15 interview questions are designed to measure applicants' ability to communicate orally, organize, prioritize, and relate to others effectively. They also measure initiative, motivation, integrity, and other skills. "This is probably the toughest part of the process," said one agent. "You have an hour to sell yourself. If you cannot, you will not make it." The three panel members will take turns asking questions. If applicants cannot think of an answer to a question, the interviewers will suggest that they move onto the next question and return to the question at the end of the interview. Applicants will not be penalized for this. If, however, they fail to answer one or more questions during the interview, this may adversely affect the outcome.

exercise. Each test has a possible grade of "low," "moderate," and "strong." A low-low or a low-moderate grade fails the applicants, a moderate-moderate grade rates the applicants as competitive, and a moderate-strong or a strong-strong rates the applicants as "most competitive."

TIPS FOR A SUCCESSFUL INTERVIEW

While applicants have no prior knowledge of the specific questions or the topics to be covered, they can

The phase II interview measures the following critical skills and abilities:

· Ability to communicate orally
· Ability to organize, plan, and prioritize
· Ability to relate effectively with others
· Ability to maintain a positive image
· Ability to evaluate information and make judgment decisions
· Initiative and motivation
· Ability to adapt to changing situations
· Integrity
· Physical requirements

get an idea of what critical skills and abilities will be measured by referring to the *FBI Special Agent Selection Process: Applicant Information Booklet* provided to each applicant early in the process. For example, one skill measured is integrity. A question may be, "Can you give me an example of how you demonstrated integrity?"

One current agent, remembering back to when he applied, said, "Even though I had a neighbor who was an FBI agent, he was not able to give me anything concrete about the test. I found out later they [applicants] all need to be on the same level playing field." There is a great deal of material published in hard copy, on the Internet, and on the FBI website about the interview process, and prior research by the applicants about the special agent position and the FBI itself should provide a good foundation for their preparation.

Greet the interviewers by shaking hands firmly, but remember it is not a strength contest, and wait until told to take a seat. Look directly at the person asking the question, and make frequent eye contact with each interviewer over the course of your answers. Sit straight, but not rigid. Avoid nervous mannerisms such as frequent crossing of the legs or fidgeting. Listen carefully to the questions and never interrupt. Speak evenly and distinctly. Use correct grammar and avoid speaking in double negatives, slang, and off-color or inappropriate language. Smile occasionally. At the end of the interview, thank the interviewers, smile, and shake hands again.

Those applicants who do not pass phase II testing will receive a letter notifying them that they may be eligible for a one-time retest one year later. Phase II testing is designed to cull out the less prepared and shows them no mercy. "In my phase II testing in Miami," said one agent, "there were 49 of us. Only nine of us made the cut."

FINAL SCREENING PROCESS

Truthfulness throughout the entire application process is vital. Any intentional false statement or willful misrepresentation will result in removal from the process. If the misrepresentation is discovered after the individual is hired, the employee may be subject to administrative or disciplinary action, including dismissal.

PERSONNEL SECURITY INTERVIEW

In addition to the structured interview, all applicants are given a personnel security interview (PSI) which will last approximately 45 minutes. This interview is also stressful. The single interviewer will ask questions concerning foreign travel and contacts, the extent of any drug usage, status of financial obligations, truthfulness of the information contained in the FD-140 application, and other security issues. Information provided during the PSI will be verified through the polygraph examination, which is generally administered on the same day. At the end of the interview, thank the interviewer, smile, and shake hands.

Director Louis Freeh (1993–2001) instituted the "bright line" policies to which all FBI employees must adhere. Certain conduct will not be tolerated, including lying, cheating, stealing, sexual harassment, and alcohol and drug abuse. To oversee these important areas, he created a new and separate Office of Professional Responsibility to deal with allegations of employee misconduct and to conduct rigorous, in-depth ethics training for FBI special agent trainees and others.

The selection process is demanding, and only the most competitive, physically fit, and motivated applicants will be successful. Of more than 11,000 applicants vying for the special agent position yearly, less than 600 will be successful. "I tell anyone thinking of a career in the FBI," said a special agent recruiter, "to major in a critical skill area, try and become proficient in a second language, and get some supervisory experience in the job market. Moreover, make sure you are in top physical condition when you come in to take the test. Then you will have an excellent chance of being competitive." *Henry M. Holden*

Prior to joining the FBI in 1985, Assistant Director Cassandra Chandler enjoyed a career as a TV news anchorperson, reporter, and talk show host for the NBC affiliate in Baton Rouge, Louisiana, and practiced law with the U.S. Army Corps of Engineers in New Orleans, Louisiana. "We have found that the men and women who express an interest in joining the FBI have the same spirit, drive, and motivation. It does not matter whether they are Ph.Ds, CPAs, engineers, or teachers; they all express a desire to make a difference and to protect America."

Special Agent Oath "[I swear] I will support and defend the Constitution of the United States against all enemies, foreign and domestic; that I will bear true faith and allegiance to the same; that I take this obligation freely, without any mental reservation or purpose of evasion; and that I will well and faithfully discharge the duties of the office on which I am about to enter. So help me God."

POLYGRAPH EXAMINATION

Each applicant who successfully completes phase II testing is required to complete a polygraph examination successfully in order to continue through the process. This exam is stressful and culls out those applicants who have been deceptive or less than truthful in their background data, including answers regarding drug use. "Even if you go into the polygraph test knowing your background is clean, and you intend to tell the truth, it is a stressful experience," said one agent. "I knew I had nothing to hide, but I was still nervous—it's the unknown, I think, that was intimidating."

Each series of questions will be administered at least three times, and the test procedure may last several hours. Repeating the questions will create a pattern for the examiner to judge truthfulness and will be the basis for a decision to advance applicants to the next phase of testing—the physical readiness test—or to reject them.

The polygraph is administered by examiners who are highly trained in interviewing and interrogation techniques. Each examiner is capable of conducting a reliable polygraph examination on issues involving criminal, national security, and employee-screening matters. Special Agents may apply for polygrapher school, and if accepted, will attend specialized training for 14 to 16 weeks at the Department of Defense Polygraphers Institute (DODPI). All federal polygraphers receive the uniform training at DODPI.

Before the actual exam, the examiner will first establish a rapport with the subjects. The examiner will ask a number of generic and unrelated questions, and determine if the applicants are physically and mentally suitable for a polygraph exam. The examiner may ask a number of standard job interview questions, such as what things are most important to the applicants in life, or questions about their upbringing. Next, the examiner will review all the questions that he or she will ask when the polygraph is administered. This is to clear up any misunderstanding about the questions and establish a common understanding of what the questions mean. The questions will cover topics such as foreign contacts, personal integrity, drug use, and falsifications on the written application.

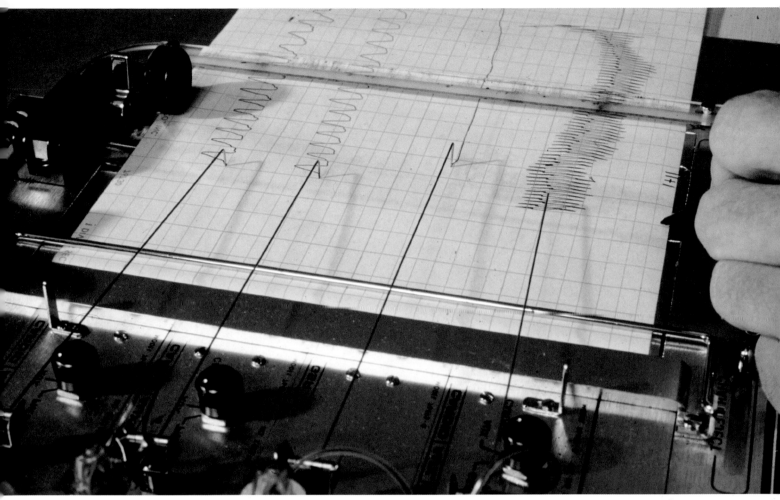

A polygraph is one tool in the special agent selection process. It is used principally to determine applicants' integrity and truthfulness on issues of national security, illegal drug use, and certain information on the FD-140 application. Like all the tests the applicants will undergo, the polygraph is serious, stressful, and may have wide implications.

Before the test, all applicants must sign a waiver, which acknowledges they are choosing to take the polygraph voluntarily and gives the FBI permission to record the interview.

CONTROL AND RELEVANT QUESTIONS

A polygraph does not detect lies but measures the physiological response to two different types of questions known as control questions and relevant questions. In order for a polygraph to work, the examiner must establish a baseline of truthful answers. This is accomplished by using control questions such as, "Is your first name James? Is the color of your hair blond? Are you sitting in a chair?" The examiner will later compare the physiological responses to those questions to what are called relevant questions in order to form a judgment.

There is no mystery to the polygraph. It records continuously, visually, permanently, and simultaneously the changes in cardiovascular, respiratory, and electrodermal (blood pressure, heart and breathing rates, and skin responses) patterns and allows the examiner to render a diagnostic opinion as to the honesty or dishonesty of each individual. "Fooling" the polygraph is not easy for someone making an untruthful response. No matter how relaxed and skilled the person is, it is difficult to control all the physiological responses that are measured. Use of countermeasures during the polygraph is grounds for discontinuing the application process.

On September 5, 2001, Robert S. Mueller III was sworn in as FBI director. On October 10, 2001, the FBI announced a new "most-wanted terrorists" list. During a press conference, Director Mueller spoke about the importance of putting the "global spotlight on those attempting to flee from justice." He also said that because of the support of the international community and of FBI legal attaché offices, four of the five international terrorists listed on the Bureau's original most-wanted fugitives list had been apprehended. One of those four, Ramzi Yousef, was the mastermind of the 1993 World Trade Center bombing and was also involved in the Manila air plot, which envisioned placing bombs on board several trans-Pacific airliners and detonating them simultaneously.

The total number of FBI employees as of September 30, 2004, was 28,904. Of that number, 12,291 were Special Agents.

Once the applicant is "on the box," as some agents call it, the examiner will go through two series of questions. The first series relates to national security issues. The topics include personal integrity and foreign contacts. The second series of questions centers on illegal drug usage and other suitability issues. The topics of questions include alcohol abuse, cheating, commission of crimes, and honesty on the application.

In general, federal law enforcement polygraph operators follow specific procedures. For each polygraph series, the examiner will collect a chart of the responses made by the applicant when asked the test questions. A brief break will be followed by the collection of a second chart of the same questions asked in a different order. The same test questions will be administered a third time, and possibly a fourth time. Any anomalies between the charts will be reviewed and the results put into the selection equation. Applicants who successfully pass the polygraph will then move on to the next phase—the physical readiness test.

EMPLOYMENT DISQUALIFIERS

There are specific behaviors that will automatically disqualify an applicant from consideration for the special agent position. They are:

- Conviction of a felony.

- Use or sale of illegal drugs (with limited exception).

- Default of student loan (insured by the United States government).

- Failure to register with the Selective Service (males only).

- A failed FBI polygraph examination regarding prior drug use, even if the extent of use would not have been disqualifying.

- A failed FBI polygraph examination regarding truthfulness on an FBI employment application.

- A failed FBI polygraph examination regarding contact with non-United States intelligence services.

PHYSICAL READINESS TEST

The job description for Special Agents specifies that they "must be fit for strenuous exertion." Special Agents may be placed in situations that make great demands on their physical capacity. In these instances, physical fitness is often the factor that spells the difference between success and failure—even life and death.

Applicants are required to pass a field office-administered physical test (PT) as a condition of employment, prior to reporting to training. The physical readiness test (PRT) will identify applicants who should be able to complete the physical training and defensive tactics portions of new agent training at the FBI Academy.

The PRT measures physical readiness in four areas. The first is a 1.5-mile run, which is scored using the following standards: 13 minutes 59 seconds or under for females and 12 minutes 24 seconds or under for males. The second is a 300-meter sprint in 52.4 seconds or under for males and 64.9 seconds or under for females. Males must also be able to perform a minimum of 38 sit-ups and 30 pushups in one minute in both exercises; females must do at least 35 sit-ups and 14 pushups. These are minimum scores that yield one point each. Applicants must score a minimum total of 12 points, based on a 40-point system. Failure to attain a passing score on this test will delay the processing of the applicants.

"I had no trouble with any of the physical requirements," said one female Special Agent. "I came from a military family and had a lifestyle of physical conditioning and sports activities in college. We give all potential applicants the physical requirements before they fill out the applications. We tell them they had better get in shape because it only gets tougher at Quantico."

More than 6,000 Special Agents have advanced degrees; more than 2,400 Special Agents are proficient in at least one foreign language.
As an example of the diversity of skills in the FBI, there are 48 chemists, three geologists, three mathematicians, and one metallurgist. In 2004, there were 3,313 Special Agents with prior military experience.

To maintain the long-cultivated public image of the FBI, applicants must be proportionate in weight and height; in other words, trim and fit. Applicants are judged on their personal appearance, hygiene, bearing, and manner. They must be able to speak logically and effectively and adapt quickly and easily to a variety of situations.

Applicants must provide a great deal of detailed information, from date and place of birth, academic achievements, employment history, and military service, to social acquaintances, foreign travel, financial status, roommates, drug use, close relatives, full-face photos, and more. Some of the information may be difficult to obtain and may require research on the part of the applicants. They should begin researching for the information as soon as possible, as there are usually no extensions for the 10-day submission period following phase I testing. "After the FBI did my background check I think they knew more about me than I did," said one agent.

FBI SPECIAL AGENT PHYSICAL FITNESS TEST PROTOCOL

Scoring Scale for One Minute of Sit-ups

Score	Males Range	Females Range
-2	31 and below	29 and below
0	32-37	30-34
1	38	35-36
2	39-42	37-40
3	43-44	41-42
4	45-47	43-46
5	48-49	47-48
6	50-51	49-50
7	52-53	51-52
8	54-55	53-54
9	56-57	55-56
10	58	57

Scoring Scale for Pushups in One Minute

Score	Males Range	Females Range
-2	19 and below	4 and below
0	20-29	5-13
1	30-32	14-18
2	33-39	19-21
3	40-43	22-26
4	44-49	27-29
5	50-53	30-32
6	54-56	33-35
7	57-60	36-38
8	61-64	39-41
9	65-70	42-44
10	over 71	over 45

Scoring Scale for 300-Meter Sprint (in seconds)

Score	Males Time Range	Females Time Range
-2	55.1 and over	67.5 and over
0	55.0-52.5	67.4-65.0
1	52.4-51.1	64.9-62.5
2	51.0-49.5	62.4-60.0
3	49.4-48.0	59.9-57.5
4	47.9-46.1	57.4-56.0
5	46.0-45.0	55.9-54.0
6	44.9-44.0	53.9-53.0
7	43.9-43.0	52.9-52.0
8	42.9-42.0	51.9-51.0
9	41.9-41.0	50.9-50.0
10	40.9 and below	49.9 and below

Scoring for the 1.5-Mile Run

Score	Males Time Range	Females Time Range
-2	13:30 and over	15:00 and over
0	13:29-12:25	14:59-14:00
1	12:24-12:15	13:59-13:35
2	12:14-11:35	13:34-13:00
3	11:34-11:10	12:59-12:30
4	11:09-10:35	12:29-11:57
5	10:34-10:15	11:56-11:35
6	10:14-9:55	11:34-11:15
7	9:54-9:35	11:14-11:06
8	9:34-9:20	11:05-10:45
9	9:19-9:00	10:44-10:35
10	8:59 and below	10:34 and below

Note: It is possible to rate a negative score in any of the four mandatory events, which will deduct that many points from the total score on the PRT. All applicants will also be required to perform pull-ups; a minimum score is not currently required for this event but may be required in the near future.

In the Adopt-A-School program, FBI volunteers encourage students to improve their academic performance and become good citizens. The program includes mentoring and tutoring programs that match socially and economically disadvantaged students with FBI volunteers acting as mentors to at-risk students while stressing getting a good education, living healthy and drug-free, and abstaining from violent and criminal behavior. All 56 FBI field offices are encouraged to "adopt" an elementary, middle, or high school in an impoverished high-crime area in their jurisdiction.

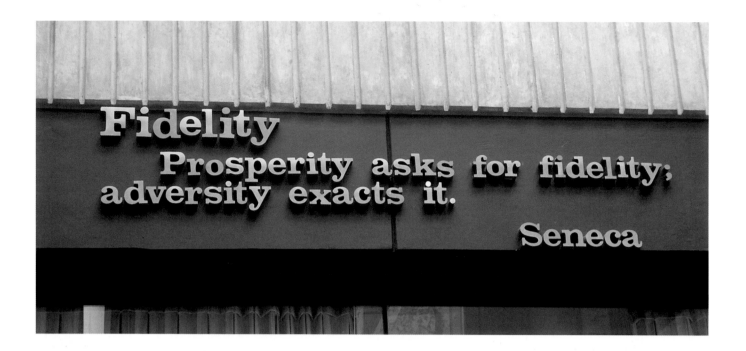

Fidelity

Prosperity asks for fidelity; adversity exacts it.

Seneca

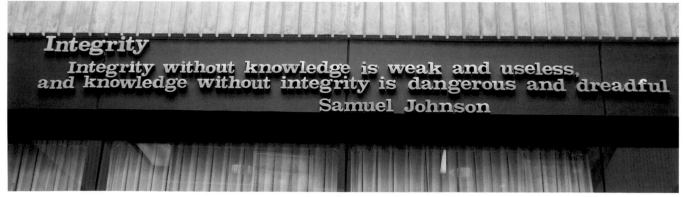

Bravery

Courage is the resistance to fear, mastery of fear not the absence of it.

Mark Twain

Integrity

Integrity without knowledge is weak and useless, and knowledge without integrity is dangerous and dreadful

Samuel Johnson

These three quotes on the walls of the FBI Academy summarize what the Bureau is about. *Henry M. Holden*

In May 1995, the Baltimore FBI office began an undercover operation—code named "innocent images"—to target people who receive and/or distribute child pornography through the use of computers and who recruit minors into illicit sexual relationships. Since then, the case has grown to become a national FBI initiative that addresses the sexual exploitation of children, particularly through the use of online computers. More than 2,000 people have been convicted to date.

BACKGROUND INVESTIGATION

All applicants at this stage will receive a full field background investigation, which includes credit and criminal background checks; interviews of associates; personal and business references; interviews of past and current employers, coworkers, and neighbors; and verification of birth, citizenship, and educational achievements. It will routinely encompass the applicants' entire lives as necessary to fully resolve any issues that may arise. "My background check took months," one agent said. "My dad was in the coast guard, and we moved 16 times when I was growing up." The background check will focus on specific areas of the applicants' history, including any arrest and driving records, as well as the applicants' character, associates, reputation, bias/prejudice, financial responsibility, alcohol abuse, illegal drug use, or prescription drug abuse.

Any unemployment or "dead time" must be included. If the length of the unemployment was significantly long, it may reflect negatively on the individual's personal initiative.

ALL-TIME TOP TEN COLLEGES PRODUCING FBI SPECIAL AGENTS AS OF SEPTEMBER 2004

University of Maryland	228
Penn State University	156
U.S. Military Academy	146
University of Texas	145
U.S. Naval Academy	139
Brigham Young University	136
California State University	130
University of California	118
State University of NY	106
University of Illinois	102

The FBI actively recruits special agent applicants at colleges around the country.

FBI AGENT DESIRABLE WEIGHT RANGES

MALES		FEMALES	
Height	**Weight**	**Height**	**Weight**
5 feet 4 inches	117–163 pounds	5 feet 0 inches	96–138 pounds
5 feet 5 inches	120–167 pounds	5 feet 1 inches	99–141 pounds
5 feet 6 inches	124–173 pounds	5 feet 2 inches	102–144 pounds
5 feet 7 inches	128–178 pounds	5 feet 3 inches	105–149 pounds
5 feet 8 inches	132–183 pounds	5 feet 4 inches	108–152 pounds
5 feet 9 inches	136–187 pounds	5 feet 5 inches	111–156 pounds
5 feet 10 inches	140–193 pounds	5 feet 6 inches	114–161 pounds
5 feet 11 inches	144–198 pounds	5 feet 7 inches	118–165 pounds
6 feet 0 inches	148–204 pounds	5 feet 8 inches	122–169 pounds
6 feet 1 inches	152–209 pounds	5 feet 9 inches	126–174 pounds
6 feet 2 inches	156–215 pounds	5 feet 10 inches	130–179 pounds
6 feet 3 inches	160–220 pounds	5 feet 11 inches	134–185 pounds
6 feet 4 inches	169–231 pounds	6 feet 0 inches	138–190 pounds
6 feet 5 inches	174–238 pounds		

Body Fat Requirements: Males—19 percent   Females—22 percent

SPECIFIC BACKGROUND CHARACTERISTICS

The background check will cover specific areas.

Character—Does the applicant exercise good judgment and discretion? Is the applicant honest and trustworthy? Is the applicant dependable, stable, and of reasonable temperament?

Associates—What types of people, groups, and organizations is the applicant involved with? Are any of those groups or organizations preaching the overthrow of the U.S. government?

Loyalty—What is the applicant's attitude and allegiance to the United States?

Ability—Does the person have the capacity or competence to perform well in an occupation?

Reputation—What is the applicant's reputation in the community and his or her place of business? Again,

the question of honesty appears: Is the person honest, and does the person display integrity among peers and associates?

Bias/Prejudice—Has the applicant exhibited an irrational attitude directed against any class of citizen or any religious, racial, gender, or ethnic group?

Financial Responsibility—This includes reviewing the applicant's credit history and assessing whether the applicant's spending habits are in line with his or her income.

Alcohol Abuse—Does the applicant use alcohol to the degree that it impacts his or her behavior?

Illegal Drug Use/Prescription Drug Abuse—Does the applicant use illegal drugs or abuse prescription medication?

FBI DRUG POLICY

All applicants in the final screening are given a urinalysis to test for illegal drug usage. A positive test will disqualify the applicant from the process. The following will also disqualify the applicant:

· An applicant who has used any illegal drug while employed in any law enforcement or prosecutorial position or while employed in a position that carries with it a high level of responsibility or public trust.

· An applicant who is discovered to have misrepresented his or her drug history in completing the application.

· An applicant who has sold any illegal drug for profit at any time.

· An applicant who has used any illegal drug (including anabolic steroids after February 27, 1991), other than marijuana, within the last 10 years *or* more than five times in one's life.

· An applicant who has used marijuana within the past three years *or* more than a total of 15 times in one's life.

PRE-EMPLOYMENT PHYSICAL EXAMINATION

The physical exam, which is provided at no cost to the applicants, consists of a complete physical, including an electrocardiogram (EKG), a clinical interview, lab work, an investigation of past or present chemical or drug dependency, and a complete blood chemistry workup. In addition, height, weight, body fat, hearing, vision, orthopedic, and neurological screening are necessary to ensure the applicants can meet the physical challenges of the wide range of work that FBI agents perform. As a result, follow-up on this process may take the longest.

If the physical examination raises medical issues or reveals conditions that require applicants to obtain additional information or undergo additional examination, it will be at the applicants' expense. Failure to provide the additional medical information promptly will cause a delay in the process and the possible deactivation of their application.

It is a long screening process, perhaps 10 to 12 months. Those who have succeeded call it "burning a seat." It is the first of several challenges still to come.

Once applicants have successfully completed the selection process, they will join a class with other new agent trainees for 17 weeks of intensive training at the FBI Academy in Quantico, Virginia.

TWO

The dormitory building and classroom complex at the FBI Academy in Quantico, Virginia, will remind a visitor of a mid-size college campus. The main training complex has three dormitory buildings, a dining hall, cafeteria, library, a classroom building, a 1,000-seat auditorium, chapel, a large gymnasium, indoor pool, firearms range, driving course, and outdoor track. *Henry M. Holden*

The Making of an FBI Special Agent

The low-key sign at the entrance to the FBI Academy understates the volume and intensity of the training that takes place beyond the front gate. *Henry M. Holden*

About an hour south of Washington, D.C., along Interstate 95 is the 60,000-acre U.S. Marine Corps base at Quantico, Virginia. Nestled in the woods surrounding the base is the 580-acre campus of the FBI Academy. The woods provide the security, the privacy, and the environment necessary to carry out training for new agents. For 17 weeks, approximately 40 to 50 young men and women—those who successfully pass the application process—will endure training challenges, unimaginable to them weeks before, in their quest to become FBI Special Agents.

FBI ACADEMY VISION

To be the premier law enforcement learning and research center and an advocate for law enforcement's best methodologies and practices worldwide.

FBI ACADEMY MISSION

To lead and inspire, through excellence in training and research, the education and development of the criminal justice community. To influence change and forge partnerships that ensure the safety and security of the citizens of the United States and around the world.

The J. Edgar Hoover reading room, located in the main library between the Washington and Madison dormitories, contains memorabilia of the longest tenured director. The main library at the academy is spacious and well stocked with the latest case law decisions and books necessary for the new agent trainees to complete their training successfully. *Henry M. Holden*

FBI ACADEMY HONOR CODE

"As a student of the FBI Academy, I devote myself to the pursuit of truth and knowledge. I subscribe to the highest standards of honesty, integrity, fidelity, and honorable behavior. I will not condone the actions of those who would use a dishonest means to attain these ethical goals."

About half of the total instruction time is in classroom lectures, presentations, and tests in law, history, counterterrorism, ethics, and more. "Integrity is the backbone of every Special Agent. Without it they will be ineffective and can be breaking the very laws they are sworn to uphold," said one agent. "There are many temptations out there. We do not make a lot of money, so the agent has to have a real commitment to the job and the Bureau. Even taking small gifts is not permitted."

In 2003, almost 900 new Special Agents graduated from the FBI Academy. In 2004, about 1,200 graduated. A new agent class begins approximately every two weeks.

GUIDING PRINCIPLES AT THE FBI ACADEMY

The training division men and women, as role models, embrace the FBI core values and are committed to excellence to our employees and all we serve. Rigorous obedience to the U.S. Constitution; respect for the dignity of all those we protect; fairness; compassion; personal and institutional integrity.

A formal intelligence officer certification can be earned through a combination of intelligence assignments and training. Once established, this certification will be a prerequisite for promotion to the level of section chief at FBI Headquarters, or Assistant Special Agent in Charge (ASAC) at the field level.

While the FBI Academy is not a military boot camp, NATs often conduct themselves in a quasi-military style. *Henry M. Holden*

SWEARING IN

All Special Agent trainees will report to Quantico on a Sunday evening. They will meet each other informally, introduce themselves, and share backgrounds. The next morning they will be sworn in as "Special Agent trainees" and will share their backgrounds with the assistant director of training and their instructors. The Special Agent trainees' backgrounds are usually as diverse as

their faces. Some were former law enforcement officers, while others were lawyers, ministers, or veterinarians. A few may speak Farsi or Arabic. Others have degrees in computer sciences, music, or military intelligence.

From the moment they step onto the base they are being evaluated for physical, academic, and "soft tangible" skills, such as being on time and helping other trainees. All new agent trainees (NATs) sign a unilaterally

New agent trainees are exposed to three components of curriculum: investigative, tactical non-investigative, and administrative. The three components total about 680 hours of instruction and spread over four major concentrations: academics, firearms, operational skills, and integrated case scenarios. The basic skills agents will need to conduct effective investigations include counterterrorism, counterintelligence, computer intrusion and fraud investigation, informant development, evidence collection and handling, human behavior, ethics, firearms, and more.

non-binding contract that acknowledges they are being observed and rated in all areas, and discloses what remedial help and retesting may be given and the standards applied to dismissal.

"There will be challenges for all of the trainees," said one instructor. "It is not supposed to be easy. The FBI has high expectations of them and we have instructors who will hold them to those expectations." Past history

and results have shown that those selected have the traits to be most successful during the training. The trainees have probably left secure, well-paying careers for a job that pays roughly $44,100 at the entry level, is not guaranteed, and in the long run, pays much less than the individual could earn in the private sector.

The training is designed to help the transition from civilian life into a life of law enforcement. "The trainee will need to set goals and give 110 percent, and stick to the program. Not too many of them who make it this far are quitters," said one instructor.

In reality, the training consumes more than 40 hours a week. "Every hour of every day is planned. We know where the trainees are always, and so do they, until the day they graduate," said one instructor.

"Our days are structured," said one NAT, "and after 5 p.m., it's up to you to put it all together." There are long nights of study, and trainees must use their own time to work on any physical improvements needed to pass the PT exams given at intervals during the training.

Over the training period, the pressure is ratcheted up to teach the NATs focus. It is a unique experience in which assignments, academics, PT, and other issues begin to pile up. Since Special Agents will juggle numerous active cases at a time, it is critical that NATs develop good time management if they are to be successful. The success rate at Quantico is high. The application vetting process and the high motivation of the individuals account for this.

HIGH ANXIETY

Anxiety is high among many of the arriving trainees. Some left secure employment for a job where they will have to prove themselves physically, mentally, and academically. All members of the new agent class will sleep on the floor in their two-bedroom suites in the dormitory. Four trainees will share a common bathroom. Each new agent trainee has a desk, computer, dresser, and single bed.

Over the course of the training period, NATs must pass nine academic examinations with a score of 85 percent or better in the following subjects: legal (two exams), behavioral science, interviewing, ethics, basic investigative techniques (pass/fail), interrogation, advanced investigative techniques (pass/fail), and forensic science. Generally, one make-up exam is allowed, but two test failures will result in a recommendation for dismissal.

During training, the candidates will receive intensive training in physical fitness, defensive tactics, practical application exercises, and the use of firearms. Those who have not physically conditioned themselves before arrival, or who lack the muscular strength and endurance necessary to cope successfully with physical encounters, will not make it through the training. Some will be culled out at the first physical fitness test, and all will be challenged in some form, especially in the early weeks. Sprained wrists or ankles or other physical injuries will account for a number of dropouts. NATs will have to learn to balance late nights and early mornings with extensive, and sometimes strenuous, physical activities.

Seventy-seven hours of training make up physical fitness and defensive tactics training. The physical training test (PT) is one of several make or break points for NATs. It is administered during the first, seventh, and 14th week of training. A minimum of 15 points out of a possible 50 is required to pass each PT test. At least one point must be scored in each of the five events as well. The five events that are tested are: pull-ups, sit-ups, pushups, 120-yard shuttle run, and two-mile run.

TRAINING BEGINS

NATs are required to reside fulltime at the FBI Academy for the first three weeks of training. After the third week, NATs may leave the academy for weekends, but must return by midnight on Sundays. NATs who do not pass an official PT test may not leave the academy overnight any night of the week, and must return to their dorm room by midnight.

The first day at the academy can be confusing, disorienting, and stressful, and that is only day one. Following the swearing in, there is a welcoming speech from the SAC, who will advise the NATs that they will perform up to Bureau standards or they will be looking for other employment. There are strict rules to follow, such as midnight curfews on weekends, no overnight stays of visitors, and no alcohol permitted in the dorm rooms. Classes will run from 8 a.m. to 5 p.m. on weekdays, 8 a.m. until noon on Saturdays, and evenings from time to time for low-light shooting, high-risk arrests, and nighttime surveillance (6 p.m. to 10 p.m.).

Part of the first day will be spent in orientation and at the academy store, where the trainees will get uniforms, textbooks, and assorted gear needed for various exercises. They will receive blue or gray jackets and tactical pants for outdoor work, and gray shirts and navy shorts for PT. Everyone at Quantico is color-coded; NATs wear blue golf shirts and khaki pants. (Drug enforcement administration (DEA) candidates, who share some of the training facilities, wear light gray.) "Everybody wears the same clothing," said one instructor. "We are building individuals into a team."

Day two will test the trainees' physical fitness. After the "weigh-in," the NATs take the physical fitness test (PFT), which consists of timed exercises. The first is the 110-yard shuttle run, beginning in a prone position. This exercise is a test of agility and assumes that the

The standard uniform required for all NATs consists of the following: knit golf shirt, tactical pants, gym shirts, gym shorts, baseball cap, chain for academy badge, a pair of running shoes or boots, rugby shirt, rain jacket, rain pants, sweatshirt, and pants. The total cost of these items is approximately $300.

agent has been knocked down and must get up and chase the fleeing suspect. A two-mile run, which is eight laps around a quarter-mile track, is next. "I was living in Las Vegas when I decided to join the FBI," said one agent. "I ran every day in my air force boots and a loaded backpack. My preparation helped me ace the FIT [PFT] test."

"Fitness is essential to succeeding," said one instructor. "Fitness gives the agent the ability to resist panic, to maintain his [or her] composure, and to exercise judgment. It is the difference between action and reaction."

Meanwhile, instructors will look for evidence of team building vital for later training. How the trainees respond to improvements suggested by instructors will say something about their independence and motivation. Some trainees lend support to others, and the sense of caring some individuals show is a reflection of the right attitude. It is the beginning of bonding necessary later for team success. "Training at the academy is not designed to fail people," said a former assistant director of Quantico. "It is not boot camp. We want and encourage everybody to succeed, and our instructors will help and encourage the trainees in every way they can."

"I felt much better about myself and my chances of being successful here after getting through that test," said one NAT.

By day three, PT will have culled out the physically unprepared trainees. Day three may be a law class where lawyers will take trainees through moot courtroom proceedings. Since FBI agents are often witnesses in court, the lawyers will simulate what NATs might face by grilling, questioning, and cross-examining all of them. The trainees will be on the hot seat, and the lawyers will hammer away at them.

Everything an FBI Special Agent does will revolve around the proper interpretation and application of the U.S. Constitution, from investigation and making proper arrests, to testifying in court and successful prosecution. Contrary to television shows depicting how arrests are made, trainees will learn that the arresting agent does not have to read the subject the Miranda warning against self-incrimination or permit the presence of legal counsel until the person is physically in custody, or restrained, and being interviewed.

The trainees will also learn that their actions as Special Agents will be forever under the microscope of review. Journalists and the public can obtain records of their

actions through the Freedom of Information Act (FOIA), and Special Agents will be under internal review, court review, and in the future, possible historical examination.

ETHICS TRAINING

Information gathering is what the FBI is about, and the methods that agents use must meet the highest standards. Among the most critical training NATs receive is law enforcement ethics. Ethics is the golden thread running through FBI training. It often is the difference between correctly applying the power of law, and conduct that may be illegal and may undermine the rule of law.

A strong foundation in ethics directs the choices and decisions that these agents will have to make every day throughout their careers, from the proper collection of evidence to questioning a suspect. "If the rule of law is to prevail," said one agent, "law enforcement must be fully supported by the public. And the public will ultimately support only those law enforcement officers, and their organizations, that are completely law-abiding."

FBI Special Agents are taught to save lives, but under certain conditions, Special Agents may have the right to take a life. For example, a violent crime has just taken place. A man has just shot a storekeeper and is fleeing the scene. Is it ethical and legal for a Special Agent to shoot the fleeing subject? The answer is yes, if the subject is still carrying a weapon. The reason is because the fleeing suspect is still a threat to the public and to the agent. It is a judgment call, for even if the subject has dropped the weapon, he may have a weapon waiting along his escape route. If practical, the pursuing agent should give a verbal warning prior to the use of deadly force. "Our policy on the use of lethal force has always been in line with the Constitution and court rulings," said one Special Agent attorney. "The seminal case leading to the policy we use began with U.S. Supreme Court's decision, *Tennessee v. Garner*, in 1985."

NATs will receive an intensive 16-hour course in ethics. Ethics matters will be reinforced throughout the entire training curriculum. Part of the ethics training is being able to distinguish the agents' role as federal law enforcement officers and as private citizens. For example, when Special Agents see the overly aggressive driver that cuts other drivers off or the obnoxious person in line at a supermarket, they cannot flash credentials and abuse their power. Civilians can elect to react, or they can move on. Special Agents must elect to move on.

At the conclusion of the training, the NAT must be able to demonstrate the application of newly learned ethical tools in actual situations in the field, using both case studies and special scenarios. In addition, the NAT must demonstrate an understanding of both moral philosophy and moral decision-making.

"I later discovered," said one agent, "that for the majority of my day-to-day duties, I relied on my training at Quantico. They taught me how to manage my resources and use good judgment. Good training, exposure, and background make for good agents," he continued. "Agents get better with experience and the guidance from senior agents."

Proper arrest techniques may be essential to agents remaining alive. "There are people out there who would not hesitate to do whatever they have to do to stay out of a pair of handcuffs," said one agent. "We have to know how to control and restrain a suspect safely; sometimes a lot is riding on how we do it." NATs are taught never to lose control of the cuffs, to always holster before cuffing someone, to always pat a suspect's pockets before reaching inside them, and to never stand in an open doorway where the backlight can make a Special Agent a perfect target.

In *Tennessee v. Garner*, 471 U.S. 1 (1985), the U.S. Supreme Court concluded: "Where the officer has probable cause to believe that the suspect poses a threat of serious physical harm, either to the officer or to others, it is not constitutionally unreasonable to prevent escape by using deadly force. Thus, if the suspect threatens the officer with a weapon or there is probable cause to believe that he has committed a crime involving the infliction or threatened infliction of serious physical harm, deadly force may be used if necessary to prevent escape, and if, where feasible, some warning has been given."

PERSONAL INTEGRITY

"A high level of personal integrity is paramount in our agents," said one senior agent. "They cannot take shortcuts even though the shortcut does not cross the line [break the law]. Throughout the training, they will see opportunities to stray, so to speak, to take shortcuts, rather than take the long road. If an agent has five witnesses to an event, and he gets pretty much the same information from four of them, he may be tempted not to 'waste his time' on the last witness, who in his mind may not have any fruitful information to harvest. He learned at the academy that it is a matter of personal integrity to do it by the book. The last witness, the one he thought may not have any useful information, could be the keystone to building his case."

Soon after arriving at the academy, the NATs will become part of an integrated case scenario. "A phone call simulating a tip to an FBI field office kicks off the integrated case scenario," said one senior agent. "We use individual lessons learned and integrate them into a scenario that has a criminal proceeding at the end of the training. They will have the opportunity to perhaps take shortcuts for right reasons, but the lessons are always about a more proper way—following the book and the rule of law."

FIREARMS TRAINING

On the first Thursday, a reality check may set in. Those who have made it to the academy have been told that they must carry their weapon while on duty and be prepared to use it. However, for some, the message may not hit home until they are actually holding the weapon in their hand, or it may be when they are told they are sitting in a seat once occupied by an agent killed in the line of duty. For others, it may be after watching graphic films of deadly shootings.

Here the shooter is rearranging the remaining rounds to have five rounds in the weapon and five rounds in the spare magazine.

FIELD OFFICE ASSIGNMENTS

About eight weeks into training, trainees will be given their field office assignments. Although trainees are given a list of all 56 field offices and asked to number their choices from one to 56, assignments will be based on the needs of the Bureau. "If the spouse is determined not to go to the assignment with the new agent, a phenomenon we call 'suicide by exam' sometimes happens," said one instructor. "The NAT has been doing well academically, and suddenly he [or she] fails two exams. He [or she] is removed from the training at that point," said one agent.

This reminder is reinforced by the frequent chatter of gunfire on a daily basis.

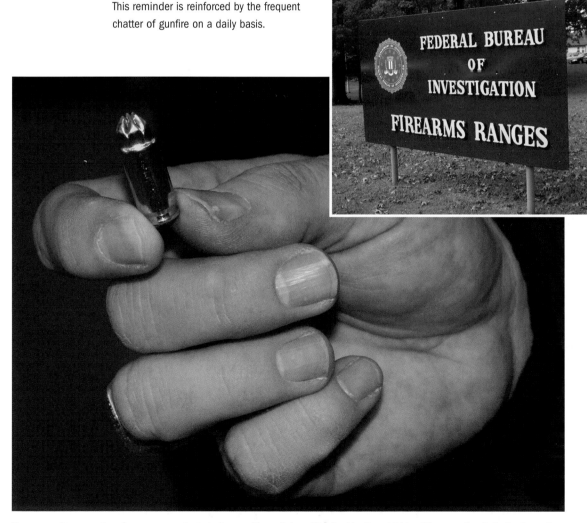

For some close-quarters firearms exercises, trainees will use "simunition," a blank cartridge with a small paintball crimped into it. The round travels at 400 feet per second, and a direct hit can break the skin. "You'll know you were 'shot,' but you'll be able to walk away and try it again," said one agent. This paintball round shatters, leaving a bright green "wound." Head, face, and throat protection is worn during these exercises. *Henry M. Holden*

Many NATs have never held a firearm in their hands, much less used it on a person, and yet they must qualify twice with the Bureau-issued Glock 22, a .40-caliber handgun, and once with the Remington Model 870 shotgun. Their first training "weapon" is a plastic Glock.

Henry M. Holden

The NATs should begin to get a sense of what their lives may be like if they graduate. This job will become a lifestyle in which they may have to use firearms to protect themselves or others. They should realize that they must commit to this lifestyle and be willing to do whatever it takes, even use deadly force, and intentionally put themselves in harm's way.

Most people are inherently unwilling to harm someone. However, as instructors will tell the NATs, there are people who will not hesitate to hurt a person, or even take a life, or do anything necessary to get away. "There are people who will want to hurt you just because you are an FBI agent. It is not personal, but it might be you. Can you deal with it?" he asks. NATs must make up their minds if they will be ready to do whatever needs to be done to stop that individual. Trainees will have to decide if they can look someone in the eyes, pull the trigger, and take a life.

They will be given the weekend to think it over. Part of their weekend assignment will be to visit the martyrs' wall and the hall of honor, and see the photos and read the names of the deceased agents. At this point, the psychological impact of shooting another human being should hit home, and a few NATs will resign. The average dropout rate from the academy is about seven to 10 percent. Generally, it is from the realization that they could never take someone's life.

SAFETY—THE PRIME DIRECTIVE

Before the NATs ever touch a live weapon, they will learn the safe handling of it; the nomenclature; how to break it down, reassemble it, and clean it safely; and the shooting standards they must meet.

Session one will come the following Tuesday when they will be issued a red plastic imitation of a Glock

Model 22, weighing approximately the same as the real weapon. The NATs will learn the proper method of receiving the weapon, removing it from its holster, and placing it in the holster. They will also learn the three cardinal rules of gun safety: treat all weapons as if they are loaded, keep your finger off the trigger unless you intend to press it, and never point a weapon at anyone unless you are justified.

One of the first things they are taught is never to cock a double-action pistol. It is too easy in the heat and adrenaline rush of a situation to discharge the firearm accidentally. The Glock is a handgun that does not have a slide safety. It requires a trigger squeeze of approximately 5 pounds to discharge the pistol.

Next, the NATs will receive a red-handled Glock. This is the real deal except that, for safety, it has its barrel blocked and its firing pin removed. NATs will practice breaking the weapon down, cleaning it, and putting it back together. There are 35 parts to the Glock, including the magazine, and this practice will extend through many evenings "after hours." Without practice, the NATs will begin to fall behind. "When the train leaves the station," said one instructor, "it only goes faster and faster. We try to help the NAT from falling too far behind, because there will be a point where he [or she] will not be able to catch up."

Even if the NAT has had prior employment in law enforcement, FBI firearms training may be a challenge. The FBI has its own way of standing and holding the weapon. "Former law enforcement habits are sometimes harder to break," said one instructor. "We teach them to shoot all over again, and for some it won't be easy. But, we never said it would be easy."

FIREARMS QUALIFICATION

Many NATs have never held a firearm in their hands, much less aimed it at a person, and yet they must pass two out of three qualification runs with the Bureau-issued Glock 22 (or 23, with a smaller handgrip), which is a .40-caliber semiautomatic handgun. Instructors will work day and night to encourage and support NATs to meet the requirements.

NATs must also qualify on the Remington 12-gauge Model 870 shotgun and demonstrate proficiency with the MP5 submachine gun. "When they leave here, NATs will be able to drive nails up to 100 yards with the MP5," said one instructor.

During training, NATs may receive a written notice of counseling from any of the academy staff for a behavior, action, or pattern of conduct that reflects a deficiency in the suitability dimensions of the NATs or otherwise reflects negatively on them. All formal counseling sessions will be documented, and NATs will sign or initial the document acknowledging that the session took place. At weeks eight through ten, a mid-course review will be conducted by the class supervisor.

Suitability dimensions include, but are not limited to: emotional maturity, conscientiousness, doing the right thing, cooperativeness, initiative, personal integrity, and good judgment. A suitability determination often involves an evaluation of all aspects of NATs' behavior and performance during training. For this reason, the determination that certain NATs are not suited for the special agent position may not occur until the final weeks of training.

Here is a small sample of the spent brass cartridges recovered from a day's shooting at one firing range. NATs will fire between 3,000 and 5,000 rounds of pistol ammunition during their training. They will also fire about 300 rounds of shotgun and 300 rounds of MP5 submachine gun ammunition.

NATs will have to demonstrate proficiency in firing a weapon with both hands. Here the NATs practice left-handed shooting. The handgun qualification course consists of four stages in which 50 rounds must be fired with a score of 80 percent (two points per hit):

Stage 1 On command the shooter will draw and fire six rounds prone position, three rounds strong side kneeling barricade position, six rounds strong side standing barricade position, and three rounds weak side kneeling barricade position. Upon completing stage I, the shooter will conduct a magazine exchange and holster a fully loaded weapon in one minute and 15 seconds.

Stage II On command the shooter will move from the 25-yard line to the 15-yard line, draw, fire two rounds in six seconds, and then stand by in position three. On command the shooter will fire four strings of two rounds in three seconds, returning to position three after each string. On completing stage II, the shooter will holster a loaded weapon.

Stage III On command the shooter will move from the 15-yard line to the 7-yard line, draw, and fire 12 rounds in 15 seconds, including a reload. On completing stage III, the shooter will holster a loaded weapon. The shooter will then rearrange the remaining 10 rounds to have five rounds in the weapon and five rounds in a spare magazine.

Stage IV On command the shooter will move to the 5-yard line, draw, and fire five rounds strong hand only, reload, transfer the weapon to the weak hand, and fire five rounds weak hand only. On completing stage IV, the shooter will unload and holster an empty weapon. *Henry M. Holden*

After the NATs have scored their targets, the instructor (in the red cap) will debrief them. *Henry M. Holden*

When NATs finish their rounds they must clear the weapon of the empty magazine, insert a loaded magazine, rise, and wait for all the shooters to finish and the range to be declared safe. Then they may advance forward of the firing line to mark and score their targets. *Henry M. Holden*

NATs must master prone shooting. The range instructors are in real-time communication with each other and the range safety officer. *Henry M. Holden*

A firearms instructor is briefing the NATs before a round of shooting on an indoor range. This class has already gone through the outdoor ranges and is near graduation. The white tape on the back of their caps is used to block out their names for the photo. *Henry M. Holden*

With over 150 law enforcement officers killed every year in the line of duty, the FBI is determined to have its agents trained to the highest standards. That is why firearms training takes up the largest block of training—28 sessions of four hours each. *Henry M. Holden*

EARLY INTERVENTION—
RECYCLINGFAST TRACK

NATs who are trying hard yet failing firearms qualification for the pistol or shotgun at the mid-term mark (approximately week nine) may be recycled once into a later new agents class, given specific one-on-one instruction, and allowed time to develop the necessary strength and skills to complete the firearms course successfully. If at the new mid-term mark they fail to qualify, recommendation for dismissal takes effect.

In addition to instructor help, there are high-tech learning aids called advanced firearms instructional techniques (AFIT) to help NATs fix a problem. NATs can wear goggles with a camera that allows the instructors to see the sight-picture the NATs are looking at, as well as other visual references. Guns can be hooked up to a graph to measure the NATs' trigger press, and cameras can record the NATs' actions in 1/16th-second frames, which allow the instructor to see the moment the NATs make mistakes.

The NATs who do not meet the standards on the final qualification (approximately week 16) will be removed from training and placed on a one-time "fast track" remedial firearms program for two weeks. If successful in the final qualification of the remedial program, the NATs will be integrated into a class and complete the training schedule. In failing this fast track, the NATs will be recommended for dismissal.

NATs will learn that warning shots, shooting guns out of people's hands ("winging" them), and other trick-shooting seen on TV is not allowed or healthy. "We don't teach them to 'shoot to kill.' We teach them to aim for the largest mass of the person and pull the trigger until the threat is eliminated," said one agent. "Because you shoot someone, it does not mean they are not going to stop what they are doing. The person will only stop what he [or

Even if the new agent trainees came from law enforcement, firearms training may be a challenge for them. The FBI has its own method of firearms instruction.

she] is doing when exsanguination takes place, when he [or she] loses enough blood from his [or her] brain." NATs will also learn that they will be scared during a gun battle. Things will happen quickly, and only about 20 percent of the rounds they fire will find the target.

FIREARMS TRAINING SIMULATION

Firearms training simulation (FATS) puts new agent trainees in simulated life-and-death situations and measures and scores their responses. FATS tracks every virtual bullet and tests the NATs' judgments and marksmanship. Computer-assisted marksmanship also assists the NATs as well as the instructors, who will use it to measure the trainees' sighting picture, rounds impacting the target, and more. FATS will aid the instructors to teach the NATs how to develop into more accurate shooters.

The simulator will present various arrest scenarios. In one, two agents are at a residence to arrest a suspect. One agent is at the front door while the other watches the suspect through a window. When the agent at the door identifies himself, the suspect reaches for a gun, raises it, and begins firing through the door. The action taken by the agent in the window determines the outcome of the scenario. Does he call "gun," draw his weapon, and fire until the suspect goes down, or does he hesitate and possibly get his partner killed?

In another scenario, the suspect is fleeing the scene of a shooting. Does the agent shoot the suspect? Are there people on the street? Could returning fire hit innocent bystanders? The interactive program scores the exercise accordingly. Of course, the NATs will be using wired guns that cannot shoot live ammunition.

This NAT is shooting at a photo of a female with a pistol in her hand. These NATs must wear their body armor and jackets at this point in their training to get used to drawing their weapon from under a jacket. Note the two brass shells ejecting from the Glock. *Henry M. Holden*

The NAT in this photo is firing weak hand unsupported. Agents must be able to shoot equally well using either hand in a number of different positions. *Henry M. Holden*

Signs warn the trainees that "hurt," "pain," and "agony" await them along the yellow brick road. The U.S. Marine Corps at Quantico designed a running course for its trainees. As a safety feature, painted yellow rocks showed runners the way through the wooded trail. Instructors told trainees to follow the yellow rocks along the way, and, soon, runners began calling the trail the "yellow brick road."

The NATs will face numerous hills that wind through rough terrain. They will soon discover that they cannot complete the course alone. Running such a demanding course usually unites and bonds the NATs, who must help each other through the tough spots. They will soon realize that the challenge is a team effort.

YELLOW BRICK ROAD

The FBI has a long-held belief that physical fitness ranks equal with mental preparedness. The "yellow brick road" course is 9 miles of wooded trails with three walls, six ropes, and 26 obstacles, making it the ultimate challenge for the trainees. They will run the course as a group and will be carefully observed by the instructors. Do the stronger trainees help the others? Does the class act as a team? These questions will allow the instructors to evaluate individuals who may perhaps be showing leadership skills, and those who may not.

LAW ENFORCEMENT COMMUNICATION UNIT

Law enforcement communication unit instructors conduct a wide variety of training. For NATs, the concentration of training is on gathering information and learning how to conduct an interview. Interviewing entails listening carefully, not talking too fast, building rapport and compassion, mirroring the subject (such as subtly repeating movements the interviewee makes), not invading a person's space, listening for human values (such as the person's religious views), and more. Informant development and field office communications will also be part of the focus of this training.

PRACTICAL APPLICATIONS

Throughout their training, the NATs will be tested through practical applications designed to measure their progress and bring out areas in need of improvement. "Practicals" measure the skills related to interviewing, collection and preservation of evidence, techniques and mechanics of arrests, defensive tactics, and other areas. Many of these practicals take place in Hogan's Alley, a training area at Quantico. "We practiced all the techniques before we got out there [Hogan's Alley]," said one NAT. "Most of the practicals were completely unexpected, but we definitely had the training for the various situations."

Serving a search warrant can be challenging for NATs. They will enter a hostile environment where distractions are made more complicated by role-players who act out crimes based on elaborate scripts. In debriefs, instructors may raise issues about the trainees' behavior that might have resulted in legal challenges in real situations. It is a continuous process of learning.

Two safe tactics and remedial training sessions will be provided to all NATs at appropriate times during the practical exercises. Failure to demonstrate a satisfactory

Among the specialized training all NATs receive are five hours of sensitivity training, 85–90 hours in Hogan's Alley, 114 hours of firearms training, 72 hours of operational skills training, 76 hours of legal training, 16 hours of ethics training, and 110 hours of counterterrorism and counterintelligence training. It costs about $50,300 to train a new Special Agent.

HOGAN'S ALLEY

ON THIS SITE IN JULY 1982, SA FELTUS B. STIRLING CONCEIVED HIS VISION FOR THE TRAINING COMPLEX WHICH WOULD BECOME HOGAN'S ALLEY. HIS VISION, INSIGHT, AND DEDICATION ARE REALIZED DAILY IN THE TRAINING EXERCISES THAT SAFEGUARD THE LIVES OF FBI AND DEA AGENTS AND OTHER LAW ENFORCEMENT OFFICERS. THROUGH THESE ACTIVITIES, HIS SPIRIT AND HIS WISDOM WILL LIVE FOREVER.

This is the Hogan's Alley dedication plaque. FBI agents are taught in lifelike conditions to prepare for real-life street crime. Hogan's Alley is a crucible for new agent trainees, for it is a place where the concentrated forces of FBI instructors and hired role players interact with future FBI Special Agents. *Henry M. Holden*

NATs practice serving a warrant under conditions they have been told may be hostile.

This series of photos shows a simulated assault on a police officer. The officer and the suspect being patted down are role players. In this scenario, the NATs drive around a corner and are confronted with the situation. *Henry M. Holden*

The instructor (in tactical shorts) moves in quickly to monitor how the NATs react. *Henry M. Holden*

While one NAT secures the suspect, a second NAT checks out the police officer, and a third covers the other two. The instructor will debrief the NATs on what they did right and what they need to improve on immediately after the exercise. *Henry M. Holden*

This advanced new agent class is practicing for shotgun qualification. Shotgun qualification course consists of firing 11 slug and five buckshot rounds and scoring 80 percent (five points per rifled slug, one point per pellet).

Stage I Starting point: 50-yard line. The shooter loads two rounds of rifled slug into the magazine and comes to position five (high ready position). On command and within 20 seconds the shooter will chamber a round, disengage the safety, and fire one round standing strong side barricade and one round kneeling strong side barricade. On completing stage I, the shooter will unload and return to position one with an empty weapon and the safety on.

Stage II Starting point: 25-yard line starting from position two with an empty weapon, action open and safety on. Within 45 seconds, the shooter must load five rounds of rifled slug, fire two rounds strong side standing barricade and three rounds strong side kneeling barricade. On completing stage II, the shooter will unload and return to position one with an empty weapon and the safety on.

Stage III Starting point: 15 yards with an empty weapon, action open and safety on, the shooter will, upon command, load four rounds of rifled slugs and fire one round in 20 seconds. The shooter moves to position three (low ready position) with safety on. On command the shooter will fire three strings of one round in three seconds, returning to position three with the safety on after each string. On completing stage III, the shooter will unload and return to position one with an empty weapon and the safety on.

Stage IV From the 7-yard line in position two with an empty weapon, action open, and safety on, the shooter will, on command, load three rounds of buckshot, fire three rounds, reload two rounds of buckshot, and fire two rounds. On completing stage IV, the shooter will return to position one with an empty weapon and the safety on.

These NATs are practicing an exercise where the suspect is hunkered down resisting arrest. Note the red-handled training weapons.

level of performance in the practical exercises will result in a recommendation for dismissal.

HOGAN'S ALLEY

Not far from the main academic complex is Hogan's Alley—a functioning town with its own zip code (22135). Its facades and buildings are primarily used for FBI (and DEA) new agent training. Trainees will confront "criminals," solve crimes, and learn to sharpen their observation skills there. Hogan's Alley includes the seedy, down-at-the-heels bar and billiard hall, the All-Med Pharmacy, the Bank of Hogan, and the Dogwood Inn, with its 30 functional rooms (where they take Visa and MasterCard), and guns *are* allowed. It is a place where NATs will confront and deal with real fear for the first time. At the time of this author's visit, room rates at the Dogwood Inn were advertised at $48 per night—a bit on the low side, but then, this *is* a high-crime neighborhood.

Across from the Dogwood Inn is the Biograph, a replica of the Chicago theater where agents gunned down John Dillinger. It has been running the same movie, *Manhattan Melodrama* with Clark Gable and Myrna Loy, for over 30 years.

The corner of State and Board Streets in Hogan's Alley, Virginia, may look like any small town in America. The quiet, almost bucolic setting is anything but that. Trainees will confront "criminals," solve crimes, and learn to sharpen their observation skills. It is a place where many trainees will confront and deal with real fear for the first time. *Henry M. Holden*

A modern version of Chicago's Biograph Theater in Hogan's Alley is often the backdrop for new agent training. *Henry M. Holden*

In 17 practical exercises, trainees will interact with staff, maintenance people, and role players hired to be the murderers, thieves, drug dealers, terrorists, and other types of people they will be up against after they graduate. However, the NATs do not know the plumber from the bank robber. The role players will try to confuse and distract the trainees. "During a practical," said one role player, "if any of the trainees let their guard down, I'm going to shoot him them." Often during practicals the trainees' respiration may become shallow, their blood pressure may go up, and perspiration may soak their shirts. It is a time to learn. "We try to scare them nearly to death here," said one instructor. "They need to face this fear in here where it is safe, learn to deal with it so when they are out on the street they can overcome it rather than getting hurt."

The unique training methods will allow NATs to apply principles they learned in the classroom, including mobile surveillance, arrest procedures, tactical street-survival techniques, high-risk building entries, and the proper use of deadly force. While every type of "criminal" has passed through Hogan's Alley, the big difference between there and the real world is that the new agent trainees do not die from their mistakes. Instead, they will walk away with a sober realization that if it had been real, they may not have returned home for dinner, or because one did not follow a procedure, another agent would have been killed.

All NATs will fire an MP5 submachine gun during their firearms course; 50 rounds (two magazines with 25 rounds) with a qualifying score of 80 percent (two points for each hit).

Stage I From the 50-yard line the shooter will load a 25-round magazine and come to position five (high ready position). With 55 seconds allotted, the shooter will, on command, chamber a round, move the selector lever to semi-auto, fire five rounds prone, and then move the selector lever to safe. The shooter will then assume the strong side kneeling barricade position, fire five rounds, then assume the strong side standing barricade position and fire five rounds. On completing stage I, the shooter will return to position one with the selector lever on safe.

Stage II From the 25-yard line, starting from position five with selector lever on safe, and with 50 seconds allotted, the shooter will, on command, fire five rounds strong side kneeling barricade, five rounds strong side standing barricade, reload, and fire five rounds weak side kneeling barricade. On completing stage II, the shooter returns to position one with the selector lever on safe.

Stage III From the 15-yard line and position three with the selector lever on safe, the shooter will, on command, fire five rounds standing and five rounds kneeling. On completing stage III, the shooter will return to position one with the selector lever on safe.

Stage IV From the 7-yard line and starting in position three, on command the shooter will fire two rounds in three seconds and return to position three. On command the shooter will fire four strings of two rounds in two seconds, returning to position three after each string. Upon completion of stage IV, the shooter will unload and return to position one with an empty weapon, bolt locked open, selector lever on safe.

Based on an actual case, the two NATs sitting in a car surveilling a building are suddenly confronted by an armed carjacker. In a previous exercise this author witnessed, the two NATs exited the car and the carjacker sped away. *Henry M. Holden*

In this exercise, two other NATs take a different approach. The driver can be seen raising his weapon to fire on the carjacker. However, the carjacker fired first, "killing" the two NATs. *Henry M. Holden*

Another part of defensive tactics training is learning to restrain a suspect safely.

In Hogan's Alley, the NATs will be taken through real-to-life training exercises such as a bank robbery (there is one almost every week), a kidnapping, an assault on a federal officer, a carjacking, and more. The trainees will also be exposed to compliant as well as armed-and-dangerous arrest scenarios.

During exercises, students will be provided with tools similar to those in the field, such as bureau vehicles, radios, and electronic surveillance equipment. "I think Hogan's Alley is where I began to feel the heart of the FBI, what the FBI is all about, and why we are here," said one agent.

OPERATIONAL SKILLS

NATs are also required to pass a defensive tactics (DT) test. "Operational skills" is an area many of the trainees have never experienced in civilian life. Most have never handcuffed and deprived freedom from a person. Here they will learn to do it safely before they go out into the real world, where one mistake can get them hurt. "We teach them: don't get killed by being stupid," said one instructor.

Defensive tactics is a misnomer. "It can be defensive at times, but at other times, when the FBI agent makes his [or her] first move, it becomes offensive," said one instructor. "DT is a combination of martial arts, street fighting, kicks, and use of chemical dispensers such as OC [pepper spray]. We don't teach them to fight fair, and we don't start a fight. The subject makes the first move. We use force when necessary to gain control or compliance," he said. "We teach them to always expect the unexpected, and when backing off is preferred."

"Not having a military background," said one NAT, "I found firearms and DT to be very challenging. I think between the two, DT was the toughest because of the variety of techniques. If I had a background in Tae Kwon Do it would have helped me during this training. You have to give your full concentration while you are here."

NATs will learn that in order to solve a problem, first they must use brainpower, then defensive tactics, and only as a last resort, deadly force. The DT test, given at approximately the 14th week, focuses on successful execution of control holds—bar hammer, arm-bar, and carotid restraint techniques—as well as baton training, handcuffing for both compliant and non-compliant subjects, searching subjects, weapons retention, and disarming subjects. A score of less than 85 points is considered a fail and indicates safety errors in the execution of arrest or self-defense techniques. A failure will result in counseling, remedial instruction, and a one-time retest within a few days of the remedial instruction. Failure of the retest will be grounds for a dismissal recommendation.

NATs in Hogan's Alley will practice realistic scenarios in a safe environment.

Traffic stops can be dangerous, and the instructors will warn the NATs to be on guard at all times.

NEW AGENT REVIEW BOARD

The New Agent Review Board (NARB) will review the trainees' progress through the academy and make determinations about NATs who are performing marginally in academics or in the physical skills. A NARB review is usually triggered by grades below a certain level or by an attitude observed by instructors. However, even though some NATs may be doing well in all the skills, there is a chance they may not graduate. The FBI culture dictates that the NATs' character or suitability must match the values of the FBI. Those NATs for whom there is a question about their suitability will go before the NARB. Information gathered by the NARB is forwarded to the section chief and special agent in charge, who ultimately decide the new agent trainee's future.

GRADUATION

After 17 weeks of study, hard work, physical fitness and weapons training, interview instruction, and more, the NATs who have successfully passed all training requirements for the special agent position are ready for one of the most rewarding days of their lives—graduation day as an FBI Special Agent. "No one part of the training was exceptionally tough," said one new agent. "But the combination of everything was almost overwhelming at times. But it took me 13 months to get here, so I wasn't about to quit."

Upon successful completion of academy training, the new agents will be sworn in and receive their badges and commission books with the credentials of FBI Special Agents. Each will be issued a Glock 22 pistol and a laptop computer. Each graduating new agents class will select one of its members to receive the Fidelity, Bravery, and Integrity Award. This is the highest award for a new Special Agent and recognizes the critical components of law enforcement ethics.

All new agents will be sworn in by the director of the FBI and serve a 24-month probationary period, which includes the four months as a NAT. During the first 12 months the new agents will be evaluated on their performance of assigned duties, and their suitability for the special agent position will be evaluated throughout the 24-month probation. (Preference-eligible military veterans will serve a 12-month probationary period.) Because all FBI Special Agents have a top-secret clearance, some may receive sensitive assignments in foreign counterintelligence or undercover work. Some may go to a large office and specialize, while others, depending on the

The fifth and final event of the physical fitness test (PFT) will be the standard pull-ups test. The score on pull-ups will not be used for pass or fail purposes. The training division will use the pull-up scores for fitness award purposes, including the 50-point award. The scoring scale for standard pull-ups is set forth below:

Scoring Scale for Pull-ups

Score	Males Range	Females Range
0	0-1	0
1	2-3	1
2	4-5	2
3	6-7	3
4	8-9	4
5	10-11	5
6	12-13	6
7	14-15	7
8	16-17	8
9	18-19	9
10	over 20	10 and over

needs of the Bureau, may go to smaller or medium size offices. All will have an opportunity to chase terrorists, spies, and criminals—at home and abroad—and the stimulation of being asked to think, to analyze, and to solve.

The new agents will have learned something about themselves during the training. They will have learned what they can and cannot handle. "I did things I never thought I could do, and I also learned when I needed to ask for help," said one agent. "You have to want to be here, or you won't make it." Many will admit that they would not have been at the graduation point without the help of the rest of their team. They will have been pushed to their mental and physical limits. They will have discovered that even when they get to a point where they think they cannot go on, they can find an inner strength to continue. "I will never forget the experiences I had in Hogan's Alley," said one agent. "And that is the point, so we don't forget the mistakes we made back there."

"We had diverse backgrounds and personalities, and still we became pretty close," said one agent. "We learned to draw on our strengths and minimize our weaknesses. And I think I will have some friends for life."

On May 8, 1972, the FBI Academy opened a new training facility on the U.S. Marine Corps base at Quantico, Virginia. Before the FBI Academy at Quantico opened, new agents trained at the old post office building in Washington, D.C. New agents would spend three weeks on the marine corps base learning how to fire weapons and make arrests.

NATs will practice high-risk building entries and will be debriefed on areas that need improvement. The FBI wants the NATs to learn from their mistakes in Hogan's Alley, not on the street.

THREE

The new 12-story Newark, New Jersey, FBI field office is state of the art. It is designed to prevent and block any potential head-on vehicle attack. The first three floors are a secure parking garage. Its front entrance is just a few yards from the bank of the Passaic River. Like most federal buildings, it has concrete and steel stanchions surrounding the building and glass that is designed to blow out rather than in on personnel.
Henry M. Holden

A Day at the Office

The father of Quantico-based Public Affairs Specialist Kurt Crawford was an FBI Special Agent in new agent class number seven in October 1963 and is his son's role model. *Henry M. Holden*

FBI Special Agents investigate violations of more than 360 federal statutes, but they did not always have this large amount of responsibility. In the early part of the twentieth century, land and mining frauds in western states were out of control. Prior to 1906, the U.S. Secret Service was the principal agency of the government that was provided with criminal investigative personnel, and few of the government departments and bureaus were equipped to adequately investigate their own internal affairs. In 1907, Attorney General Charles J. Bonaparte advised Congress that the Department of Justice had no "detective force" under its immediate control to pursue federal crimes.

Today, the FBI is the primary law enforcement agency for the U.S. government. Over the years, its investigative jurisdiction has expanded to include the following: train robberies, copyright violations, enforcing the Mann Act (which forbids the transportation of women across state lines for immoral purposes), forgery, kidnapping, civil rights violations, organized crime, crimes on aircraft, sports bribery, and more.

Here is a portion of the fingerprint file section of the identification division of the FBI around 1940. This is where the fingerprint impressions of criminals were compared. Notice only one individual in the room seems to be "out of uniform."

Seventy years ago the Bureau of Investigation created a technical laboratory in room 802 in the Southern Railway Building in Washington, D.C. It was initially equipped with only a microscope (which cost $590), ultraviolet light equipment, a helixometer (a device to measure the bore or interior of a gun barrel), and a drawing board. Note the air conditioning device on the far right wall.

This early photo of the FBI serology laboratory shows the basic technical equipment of the day in the foreground.

This 1940s photo shows that fingerprint technology used only a basic magnifying glass to analyze fingerprints. In those days the FBI had three processes for detecting fingerprints. Today it has more than 80.

Preliminary fingerprint classification takes place on incoming fingerprint cards by the classifying unit of the technical division. In this 1950s photo, the dress code seems to have been slightly eased, since all the personnel are sans vests.

Part of the old photographic unit, these agents are processing photographic prints. Today much of this effort is controlled by computers.

The FBI's mandate is the broadest of all federal investigative agencies. It can investigate all federal criminal violations that are not specifically assigned by Congress to another federal agency. "No matter what we are investigating," said one agent, "civil rights, terrorism, foreign intelligence, organized crime, drugs, violent crimes, or a financial crime, our job is to examine the evidence and discover the truth."

FBI Special Agents have an obligation to both the public and the accused to provide equal justice. An agent may have all the evidence pointing to one individual, and this is where their training makes the difference. The facts sometimes reveal that the accused is innocent. New

> The FBI is the primary federal agency responsible for investigating all allegations of violations of federal civil rights laws.

Newark Division Special Agent in Charge Joseph Billy, Jr., an FBI veteran of more than 20 years, confers with Special Agent Stephen Kodak. SAC Billy served in counterterrorism, and as Assistant Special Agent in Charge (ASAC) of the FBI Academy at Quantico, Virginia. SA Kodak joined the FBI at the age of 35 after a successful career as a U.S. Marine Corps officer. *Henry M. Holden*

agents being to develop their skills to seek the truth at Quantico and continue development on the job.

AFTER QUANTICO

The generalist theory of FBI training, first created by J. Edgar Hoover, has endured the test of time and is used today. FBI Special Agents receive broad training that allows them to shift almost seamlessly from one type of crime to another, as the needs of the Bureau change. Whether it is terrorism, white-collar crime, or espionage, because of the training, all FBI Special Agents can be instantaneously deployed to any crisis and to work any program effectively.

"Our training gives us the ability to move agents from one discipline—say white-collar crime—to counterterrorism without the agent standing down for new training," said one agent. Most "street agent" work is basic police work—establishing rapport, interviewing witnesses, interrogating suspects, recording information, and researching. "It is deductive reasoning," said one agent. "Putting the pieces of the puzzle together, or connecting the dots." These techniques apply to all aspects of a criminal investigation. "For several weeks after 9/11, we pulled agents from other squads to investigate the terrorist attacks, to conduct field interviews, and feed the information back to our intelligence people," said one senior agent.

> Financial crimes are often called "white-collar" crimes. The FBI categorizes white-collar crimes as those illegal acts characterized by deceit, concealment, or violation of trust, and which are not dependent upon the application or threat of physical force or violence. These include healthcare fraud, Internet fraud, banking fraud, and money laundering, to name a few.

> In 1939, President Franklin D. Roosevelt assigned responsibility for investigating espionage, sabotage, and other subversive activities jointly to the FBI, the Military Intelligence Service of the War Department (MID), and the Office of Naval Intelligence (ONI).

After graduating from Quantico, Special Agents may choose to obtain certification in a variety of unique areas, such as Special Agent bomb technicians, special weapons and tactics (SWAT), cryptanalysis, emergency response technicians, the FBI disaster squad, or as members of the elite hostage rescue team.

During the two-year probation period, new agents' responsibilities gradually increase. They attend regular classes in areas that will continue to increase their law enforcement knowledge base and physical skills. These classes and seminars will include crime scene photography, credit card fraud investigation, counterintelligence, and counterterrorism, to name a few. In general, supervising Special Agents teach the subjects in which they have experience. In addition, all Special Agents attend law seminars four times a year to stay current on changes to legislation, new legal interpretations of laws, and new statutes, to equip them with the knowledge to perform their duties in a legal and ethical manner.

About 50 pounds of ammonium nitrate and fuel oil destroyed this vehicle. The car was blown apart as a part of a large-vehicle bomb post-blast investigation class. The FBI trains bomb technicians worldwide in the post-blast investigation process.

There are various ways to develop latent prints. Some latent prints still require the old method of dusting to make them visible, but modern chemicals and fluorescent materials do a superior job in capturing impressions that would otherwise be lost. April 3, 1978, marked the first successful use of lasers to detect latent prints on case evidence by the FBI laboratory division. Mylar—the material used for party balloons—when subjected to an electrostatic charge may also yield impressions unseen by the naked eye.

FIRST ASSIGNMENT

The SAC at the new agents' first office will review their background, training evaluations, and strengths and weaknesses, and decide where to assign each new agent within the office. The new agents may be assigned to a specific squad with specific assignments, such as healthcare fraud or counterterrorism squad.

"We try to place our new agents in small to medium size offices so they can work a variety of cases before specializing in certain programs or investigative background areas," said one senior agent.

Generally, some new agents will spend three to six months performing FBI applicant background checks. This will give them opportunities to hone the interviewing skills they first learned at Quantico. The agent will interview neighbors and friends of the applicants, and then move on to former employers, teachers, and coworkers.

Other new agents will work the applicant squad doing background checks on potential White House employees, interviewing the applicants' relatives, and reviewing their financial records. Others may work in a field office special operations unit on surveillance.

HEALTHCARE FRAUD

Many of the FBI's 56 field offices rank healthcare fraud as their number one white-collar crime problem. Healthcare fraud is so rampant that every FBI field office is investigating offenses, and many of the larger offices have squads of agents whose sole responsibility is to pursue these cases. One of the primary missions of the healthcare fraud unit, established in 1993, is to ensure the success of investigations, which have a national impact on the healthcare fraud crime problem. Many of the players in health care fraud schemes are not the seedy criminal type. They are people one would never expect to be criminals: doctors and pharmacists, nurses and physical therapists. "We accomplish our mission by concentrating our investigative resources on large healthcare corporations suspected of committing fraud against both public and private payers of healthcare benefits," said one agent, "and by coordinating these investigations with other law enforcement agencies."

In July 2001, the FBI's Kansas City division discovered that Robert Courtney, a pharmacist, was diluting doses of Gemzar and Taxol, two chemotherapy drugs used to treat cancer patients. Agents set up a sting operation to purchase drugs from Courtney's pharmacy and sent approximately six prescriptions to the U.S. Food and Drug Administration for testing. The tests showed that prescriptions prepared by Courtney, which should have had 100 percent of the prescribed drugs, actually had anywhere from 39 percent to less than 1 percent of the cancer drug.

On August 23, 2001, Courtney pleaded guilty to eight counts of tampering involving serious bodily injury and twelve counts of adulteration/misbranding. He agreed to accept a sentence of between 17 1/2 years and 30 years in prison, to forfeit all of his property, and to provide the government with a full accounting of all his criminal activities and the criminal activity of any other individuals involved.

In another case, a retired FBI agent went undercover in a nursing home to document a similar fraud. "We outfitted the retired agent with a small, false chest cavity from which we had a tube extending where the doctor could inject the 'patient's' medication," said an agent. "A doctor at the nursing home had been diluting medicine and overcharging Medicare up to five times more for medication not used.

"Thanks to modern latex materials and makeup, the doctor never realized he was administering the diluted medicine into a holding capsule within the false chest cavity. I believe he is still thinking about the error of his ways from a federal prison cell."

After approximately three years, agents may be transferred to a larger field office where they will specialize in one of four program areas—intelligence, counterterrorism/counterintelligence, cyber, or criminal—and will receive advanced training tailored to their area of specialization.

The Bureau's strength lies in its ability to gather and connect bits of vital information. "We want people who can write it down and develop critical thinking skills—people who enjoy exercising their minds," said one senior agent. "We want individuals who are naturally curious and have an appetite to learn." The Bureau looks for men and women who are self-starters. "Most of the new agents we get are people who don't need to be told to get to work. They have the ability to task themselves and do whatever is required. They are aggressive, but know when to back off and work as a team, and they also understand they are responsible for the investigations in their caseloads."

Special Agent James Margolin spent seven years as a Wall Street lawyer before joining the FBI. "I was single at the time, 32 years old, and had saved some money, so the pay cut I took did not bother me," he said. "I enjoyed the Quantico experience. I had always been a runner and swimmer, and for 16 weeks it was fun to get back into the academic environment." *Henry M. Holden*

The FBI's applicant program manages background investigations on all persons who apply for positions with the Department of Energy, the Nuclear Regulatory Commission, the Department of Justice, and the FBI. It also conducts background checks for presidential appointees, White House staff candidates, and United States court candidates.

Among perpetrators of Internet crimes, in which the FBI has jurisdiction, nearly four in five (79 percent) are male and half reside in one of the following states: California, New York, Florida, Texas, and Illinois. While most are from the United States, perpetrators also have a representation in Nigeria, Canada, South Africa, and Romania. E-mail and web pages are the two primary mechanisms by which the fraudulent contact takes place. In all, 66 percent of complainants reported they had e-mail contact with the perpetrator and 18.7 percent had contact through a web page.

On September 20, 2004, the FBI National Instant Criminal Background Check System (NICS) processed the 50 millionth background check. That check originated from a Texas gun dealer who had an outstanding warrant for aggravated assault, which was posted on the system. An FBI NICS employee contacted the sheriff's office, who verified the warrant was active and, based upon the NICS notification, apprehended the subject. The individual had been arrested previously on various charges, including aggravated kidnapping and aggravated assault with a deadly weapon.

The FBI works with other law enforcement agencies to dismantle illegal drug operations. Dismantlement means the targeted organization is permanently rendered incapable of distributing drugs. At a minimum, this requires that the organization's leaders are completely incapacitated, its financial base is destroyed, and its drug supply connection and network are irreparably disrupted. *Immigration and Customs Enforcement Agency (ICE)*

Here is part of the massive collection of the reference fired specimen file. The unit maintains the firearms collection, which contains over 6,000 handguns and shoulder firearms, and a standard ammunition file, with a collection of over 15,000 military and commercial ammunition specimens of foreign and domestic manufacture. This is not a gun museum, but a working collection.

Almost immediately after the breakup of the space shuttle *Columbia* upon reentry, FBI evidence response teams, hazardous material response teams, special agent bomb technicians, and an FBI dive team weredeployed to work with the National Aeronautics and Space Administration (NASA). The coast guard maneuvers a small boat closer to the shoreline while a member of the FBI dive team scans the shore for debris from the shuttle. *U.S. Coast Guard*

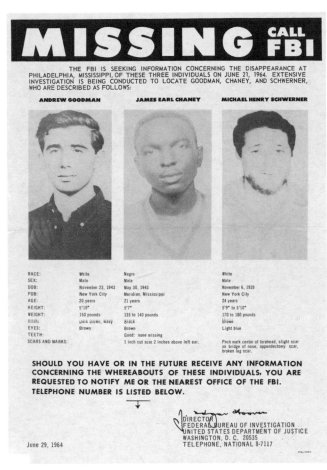

In 1964, James Chaney, a 21-year-old black man from Mississippi, Andrew Goodman, 20, and a 24-year-old Jewish man, Michael Schwerner—both white men from New York City—were in racially segregated Mississippi to help organize black voter education and registration campaigns opposed by groups such as the Ku Klux Klan. They disappeared within 24 hours of their arrival in the state. Their bodies were found five weeks later in an earthen dam near Philadelphia, Mississippi. Eventually, 19 men, including the county sheriff and a deputy, were convicted of federal conspiracy charges in connection with the murders.

To prepare for an arrest, the Special Agent must prepare an arrest plan outlining the details of the arrest, including the subject, time, place, backup agents, a list of nearby hospitals and emergency responders, and other vital information. Depending on the size of the investigation, the plan may be approved by the squad supervisor or it may require the review and approval of the Assistant Special Agent in Charge (ASAC) or Special Agent in Charge (SAC).

All Special Agents have the opportunity to volunteer to become certified as a defensive tactics instructor. The two-week course in Quantico is physically taxing. First, agents must undergo the physical test (PT), but to a higher standard than other agents, and then take the instructor certification course.

Director Hoover had a long-standing policy that prohibited agents from going undercover, and as a result, undercover operations were virtually nonexistent during the Hoover years. His preferred method of obtaining information was through paid informants and wiretaps

INTERVIEWING SKILLS

Even complicated cases revolve around basic investigative tools; one is interviewing witnesses. FBI Special Agents are trained to treat everyone, suspects and witnesses, with respect. "If we treat everyone with respect, those who have something to hide will eventually let their guard down and tell us what we want to know," said one agent.

"We have learned through situations and time that there are some really bad people in the world," he said. "But we also learn that there are some good people who make bad choices. Learning to assess an individual properly comes from training and experience. Often the person we are interviewing initially is not a suspect in the crime. However, if during the interview he [or she] sees we are getting close to figuring him [or her] out, it could turn ugly. We need to be in good physical condition," he continued, "good with a weapon, and think ahead to the possibilities of what could happen during an interview, be ready and handle it accordingly."

The FBI must investigate every threat they get. "Even if we know a person was for a moment upset—let's say with the government—we interview the person, and we have to decide if they are telling the truth or not, and do they pose a future threat? The agent will have to decide if the person deserves an admonishment, or if we should be doing more, perhaps putting the individual under surveillance."

The FBI Special Agents' ability to detect lies or deceptive behavior during an interview or interrogation depends on their ability to observe, record, and differentiate what they witness. They learn to identify clusters of behavior and nonverbal clues and to decipher their meanings.

Taking a suspect into custody can be dangerous, and FBI agents must train for such an event until they have it perfect. Having a partner makes it less dangerous, but still the agents must not let their guard down.

READING NONVERBAL SIGNALS

The only certain method of determining the truth relies on the collection of the known facts, independent of the information provided by the person interviewed. However, Special Agents will learn to carefully observe individuals being interviewed in order to gain insight into their honesty. Special Agents cannot prevent people from lying, however they can observe and record behaviors that indicate, but do not necessarily conclude, dishonesty. The more observations of the individuals the agents can make, the more accurately they can form an opinion about the candidness of the individuals.

FBI Special Agents will routinely look for nonverbal signals to determine if people are not being truthful. Left-handed people usually look to the left when lying. Right-handed people looking to the left may be searching their memory section of the brain for the truthful answer. When looking right, they may be trying to create information or lie.

Actions such as individuals angling their body away from the interviewer, shifting eyes and avoiding eye contact, and rubbing their throat as if trying to squeeze the words up their neck to get them out are all signs that they may not be telling the truth. People who attempt to conceal information often breathe faster, taking a series of short breaths, followed by one long deep breath.

"Lying requires the individual to keep facts straight, yet make the story believable enough to withstand scrutiny," said one agent. Usually one lie requires backup with another lie. Dishonest people prefer concealing the truth rather than making up fictitious stories. In other words, liars convey the truth up to the event they want to hide. At this point, they use a "text bridge" to avoid the concealed activity. After crossing this sensitive area, they relay the truth again. The use of text bridges alerts the Special Agent to a topic that may require closer examination.

Special Agents will construct and ask specific questions to facilitate specific behavioral reaction or body language. The more the agents observe the individuals being questioned, the greater the chance they will detect any lies. Family members and close friends generally display patterns of genuine openness. For new Special Agents, these patterns will often serve as a baseline reference to contrast with deceptive patterns.

"When individuals tell the truth, they often make every effort to ensure that other people understand. In contrast, liars attempt to manage the agent's perceptions. As a result, people unwittingly signal deception via nonverbal cues," said one agent. However, no single nonverbal cue is evidence of deception. It only serves as an indicator of possible deception."

Some commonly used text bridges include "I don't remember," "the next thing I knew," "later on," "shortly thereafter," "afterwards," "after that," "while," "even though," "when," "then," "besides," "consequently," "finally," "however," and "before."

The FBI provides a rapid investigative response to reported federal crimes involving child victims, such as kidnappings, sexual assaults, sexual exploitation, international parental kidnappings, and Child Support Recovery Act matters.

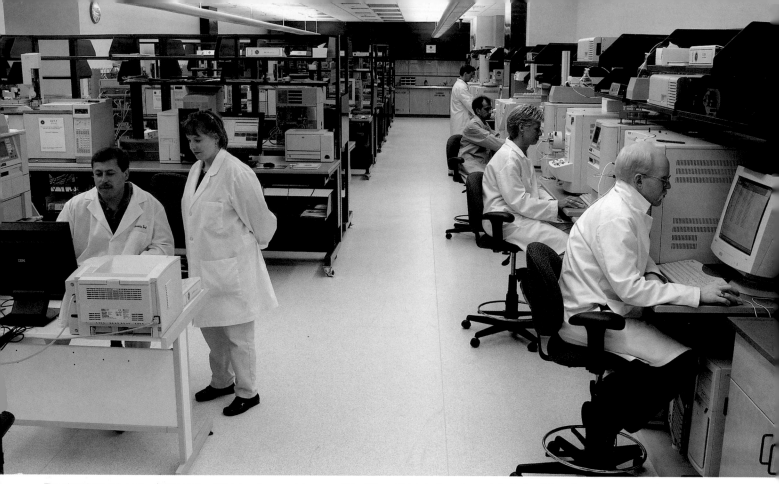

The chemistry lab in the $150 million FBI laboratory contains over $3 million of high-tech equipment, including infrared spectrometry equipment.

Some of the professional support employees in the FBI laboratories include experienced scientists, cryptologists, and engineers.

In 1968 African American civil rights leader Reverend Dr. Martin Luther King, Jr., was assassinated in Memphis, Tennessee. At the time, the FBI lacked jurisdiction in what was a local crime. Attorney General Ramsey Clark ordered the FBI to investigate the shooting. Over 3,000 Special Agents were eventually involved in tracking leads that led to the identity, arrest, and conviction of the killer.

Two months after the assassination of Dr. King, Senator Robert F. Kennedy was shot and killed in Los Angeles after winning the Democratic primary in California. Attorney General Ramsey Clark invoked the 1964 Civil Rights Act and the 1965 Voting Rights Act to bring the FBI into the case. Provisions of these acts made it a federal crime to injure persons campaigning for public office.

NATIONAL CRIME INFORMATION CENTER

The FBI's National Crime Information Center (NCIC), established in 1967, is a nationwide computerized index of information on crimes and criminals. It includes locator-type files on missing and unidentified persons, fugitives, and stolen property. NCIC averages 3.5 million transactions per day and is accessed by law enforcement and criminal justice agencies.

NCIC CASE FILE STATISTICS: AS OF AUGUST 15, 2004

Stolen vehicles: 892,536
Wanted persons: 1,137,178
Missing persons: 105,055
Stolen guns: 2,470,893
Unidentified persons: 57,002
Total number of files in NCIC: 8,683,695

Fingerprints: Total (2004) 16,109,777—
Criminal (8,317,203),
Civil (7,792,574)
Daily average number of receipts: Total 50,343—
Criminal (25,991),
Civil (24,352)
Receipts as a percent of the total:
criminal 52 percent, civil 48 percent

Electronic Processing Performance
for Fiscal Year 2004:
Criminal percent completed within two hours:
94.4 percent
Civil percent completed within 24 hours:
99.2 percent

The hazardous materials response unit (HMRU) team members demonstrate the decontamination process in their "moon suits." The unit was established in 1996 in response to the threat of terrorism involving chemical, biological, and nuclear weapons and to an expanding caseload of environmental crimes. The field offices also have hazardous materials response teams (HMRT). Currently there are 27 teams in the 56 field offices.

Forensic toxicology is a highly sophisticated science that uses a range of scientific analyses to identify and quantify foreign substances in the body and the environment that can have a toxic or behavior-altering effect, and then takes those analyses to courts of law. The science of forensic toxicology grew out of murder by poisoning. Nearly 200 years ago French scientist M. J. B. Orfila began to systematically study poisons and to isolate arsenic from autopsy samples.

INTERVIEW AND INTERROGATION

The interview and interrogation are two unique tools the Special Agent uses to seek the truth. The interview is a dialogue with an individual. The purpose of an interrogation is not to gain a confession; instead, it is a process to discover the truth.

Through interviews, agents can learn about the subjects' needs, fears, concerns, and attitudes. Interview questions should be open ended, giving subjects a chance to tell something about themselves. It may be as simple as "Can you tell me about your day?" The questions should develop rapport. Closed-ended questions tend to elicit "yes" or "no" responses, which generally do not yield much information. "People will generally talk if they trust you," said one agent. "Rapport builds trust, and trust leads to disclosure."

Every interrogation should be preceded by an interview. Special Agents will use the interview information to prepare questions to use during the interrogation. Interviews may help agents determine if certain subjects should be interrogated early or late in the day and whether they should use a hard or soft approach. Through non-threatening initial inquiries, investigators can identify nonverbal and verbal cues exhibited by the subjects, build rapport, find common ground with them, and determine if an interrogation will gain additional facts. There should be no interrogation if the agents doubt that the subjects were involved in the crime.

In Quantico, the NATs learned the standards for interviewing and interrogations. Now, in the real world, it is no longer practice. The agents may have to take people into custody and deprive them of their freedom. "It is serious and it is important that we proceed with respect to the law," said one senior agent.

"When we interrogate someone, the individual may not be in custody," said one agent. "We have shifted the line of questioning to a higher level." If the person is in custody—that is, restrained—the interrogation must be preceded by reading the Miranda warning. But, "in custody" is also a matter of perception, so the decision of whether to read a Miranda warning may also be based on common sense. Would a reasonable person see the individual as in custody even though he or she was not physically restrained? Does the individual perceive him- or herself to be in custody? If yes, then a Miranda warning is appropriate before an interrogation.

THE FBI'S TEN TOP INVESTIGATIVE PRIORITIES:

1) Protect the United States from terrorist attack.
2) Protect the United States against foreign intelligence operations and espionage.
3) Protect the United States against cyber-based attacks and high-technology crimes.
4) Combat public corruption at all levels.
5) Protect civil rights.
6) Combat transnational and national criminal organizations and enterprises.
7) Combat major white-collar crime.
8) Combat significant violent crime.
9) Support federal, state, county, municipal, and international partners.
10) Upgrade technology to successfully perform the FBI's mission.

MIRANDA WARNING

"You have the right to remain silent. Anything you say can and will be used against you in a court of law. You have the right to speak to an attorney, and to have an attorney present during any questioning. If you cannot afford a lawyer, one will be provided for you at government expense. Do you understand these rights?

"If you decide to answer questions now without an attorney present you will still have the right to stop answering at any time until you talk to an attorney. Do you understand?

"Knowing and understanding your rights as I have explained them to you, are you willing to answer my questions without an attorney present?"

RECORDING THE FACTS

While interviewing and interrogating individuals is essential to discovering the truth, the FBI's written record of all the relevant facts is equally important. The record must have all the known facts of the case, such as time, date, any witnesses, and the location of the crime. The account should also record the description and condition of the crime scene. Was it raining or snowing, clear or foggy? Was it daytime or nighttime? Did the crime scene look "fresh," or could the crime have been committed days or weeks ago? The team will also make still and video photos, and draw sketches of the crime scene. The photographs are important, for they will help refresh the agents' memories about details of the crime and serve as evidence if the case goes to court. All documents, photos, sketches, film, audio or written interviews, and agents' notes go into a case file. The team will double-check their notes, photos, and sketches to ensure they have a complete picture before they release the crime scene.

SURVEILLANCE

Second only to operating confidential sources, surveillance is one of the most frequently employed investigative techniques in obtaining arrests, indictments, and convictions for the FBI. Unlike using informants, however, conducting surveillance—whether it is distant or close up—requires using the team concept. Undercover (UC) work for some FBI Special Agents is exciting, sometimes fun, and often filled with danger.

FBI Special Agents are trained to conduct many different types of surveillance. Investigators always should assume that subjects engaged in operational, terrorist, or criminal activity will attempt to detect surveillance by employing a variety of methods and techniques. For example, as part of al Qaeda's specialized training, operatives are instructed to follow meticulous operational security. Tactics include conducting dry runs prior to becoming operational, using secondary roads and public transportation to flush out surveillance, and employing prearranged signals to communicate the absence or presence of surveillance to other al Qaeda members.

"Some of my fondest memories and fun days took place when I was undercover," said one senior agent. "We got a tip that a suspect in one of our cases was about to flee the country. He had been recognized at the airport and we sent some agents to arrest him. Since he was in a crowded public place, we had to be careful not to involve civilians. It was a terminal concourse where the airlines had their counters in one long row. I was watching him jump from airline to airline buying one-way tickets to different cities. He was trying to confuse anyone who was tailing him. We thought he made some of the UC guys, and they dropped off the surveillance since it might lead to a violent confrontation in a public place if they moved in. Here I was in my 'Bahama Mama' T-shirt, shorts, sunglasses, and floppy hat. I looked like I was going on vacation. The suspect never once looked at me because it never entered his mind that a tall, black female could be an FBI agent.

"Finally, he made for one of the gates, and I was right behind him, radioing the rest of the team where he was headed. They would arrest him before he boarded the plane.

All Special Agents who work surveillance will take the tactical emergency vehicle operators course (TEVOC). This course teaches agents defensive driving and emergency vehicle operation techniques. Part of the course requires the agent to drive as fast as possible through a precision obstacle course. The course is 0.9 mile and has 18 obstacle cones. Mobile surveillance is one of the most difficult types to carry out. Agents will work as a team, with at least three cars. One will act as the "trigger," being close enough to identify the target but far enough away not to be noticed. The second car will park in an area not in sight of the suspect. This car may cover one of the suspect's directions of travel. The third car may cover another of the suspect's possible directions of travel. Mobile surveillance cannot work without radio communication between the surveillance team. When the suspect moves, the trigger will communicate the suspect's direction, speed, any unusual driving tactics, and loss of contact. Ideally, and depending on the suspect's direction, one of the team members will pick up the "eyeball," or lead vehicle, while the rest of the team will be in strategic positions or part of the surveillance convoy. To avoid the suspect becoming aware he or she is being followed, the team car may hand off the eyeball position to another team car.

Latex gloves and crime scene templates are a part of every crime scene investigation.

"He gets to the gate, and suddenly turns around and looks straight at me. He gets this look on his face like 'Where have I seen you before?' A dangerous situation can develop at any time, so before he could react, I grabbed a public phone and pretended I was making a call. He was still staring at me, trying to place where he had seen me, and I knew this could go bad very quickly. The plane at the gate was deplaning its passengers, and I saw a tall, black man coming off the plane. Now, this is where it could have gotten worse. I hurried up to the man, greeted him like an old friend, took his arm, and turned him away from the suspect so he could not see the baffled look on my new 'friend.' As I walked away arm-in-arm with this total stranger I explained I was an FBI agent undercover. The suspect concluded I was only waiting for a passenger and went forward in boarding the plane I had identified. The FBI was waiting for him when his plane landed.

"We're taught to evaluate a situation and make a judgment. In this case, there was no time to debate or call for help. I never saw that gentleman [the debarking passenger] again, and I wonder if he is still thinking, 'What the heck was going on back there?'"

TRANSNATIONAL CRIMINAL ENTERPRISES

The FBI came of age in a time of turmoil in America—during the Great Depression and the beginning of organized crime. The FBI's fight against modern organized crime is unlike other criminal investigation programs. Instead of focusing on the crimes as individual events, the FBI's transnational criminal enterprises program targets the entire organization responsible for the criminal activities. It is called the enterprise theory of investigation. This mission is accomplished through sustained, coordinated intelligence-driven investigations and the use of criminal and civil provisions in the Racketeer Influenced and Corrupt Organization (RICO) statute.

"One of the FBI's top 10 priorities is transnational criminal enterprises, and drug trafficking is one of those enterprises," said one senior agent. "Under the banner of transnational criminal enterprises, you'll find money laundering, stock market manipulation, alien smuggling, human trafficking, document fraud, drugs, and narco-terrorism, to name a few for which we can use the RICO model to take them down.

"Narco-terrorism is fueled by drug money, and it is used to fund political assassinations and long-term terror and unrest in a country. There are links between all these terrorists' activities, such as the Revolutionary Armed Forces of Colombia (FARC), the National Liberation Army (ELN), the Shining Path [Sendero Luminoso], and a strong Middle Eastern presence on the Colombian, Ecuadorian, and Peruvian borders in South America. We have to determine the extent of those links and how they affect our national security."

These transnational criminal enterprises include traditional, well-entrenched organizations such as La Cosa Nostra and Italian organized crime, Eurasian organized crime, African criminal enterprises, Balkan organized criminal enterprises, and Asian criminal enterprises.

On April 9, 1984, the Department of Justice announced charges in the "pizza connection" case. FBI agents and Italian law enforcement officials documented international connections between American and Italian organized crime groups in a large heroin distribution ring. Eighteen men were convicted, including five organized crime family leaders.

On January 28, 1982, at the direction of Attorney General William French Smith, the administrator of the Drug Enforcement Administration (DEA) began reporting to the director of the FBI. The FBI and DEA were given concurrent jurisdiction over narcotics violations and have worked together on these matters since that time.

FBI CORE VALUES

FBI employees must uphold and revere core values that include integrity, reliability, and trustworthiness. Any employee whose conduct is at odds with these core values forfeits his or her right to FBI employment. At the same time, there is firm discipline for lesser incidents of misconduct. Some (but not all) behavior for which employees can be dismissed includes:

· Lying under oath.
· Failure to cooperate during an administrative inquiry when required to do so by law or regulation.
· Voucher fraud.
· Theft or other unauthorized taking, using, or diversion of government funds or property.
· Material falsification of investigative activity and/or reporting.
· Falsification of documentation relating to the disbursement/expenditure of government funds.
· Unauthorized disclosure of classified, sensitive, Grand Jury, or Title III material.

The FBI plans long term and targets entire organizations, rather than specific individuals, as does local law enforcement. "We pursue targets which have direct ties to significant national and international criminal enterprises, and systematically take those enterprises apart," said one agent. "We also have to remain flexible enough to pursue regional organized crime groups who are conducting significant racketeering activity; and we must ensure that our targets are permanently dismantled or significantly disrupted."

THE BRIGHT LINE POLICY

In 1994, the "bright line" policy was created to place an emphasis on the integrity and independence of the FBI. The bright line policy puts all employees on notice as to what is expected of them. It emphasizes that certain conduct such as lying, cheating, stealing, sexual harassment, and alcohol and drug abuse will not be tolerated. To oversee these important areas, the FBI created a separate Office of Professional Responsibility to deal with allegations of employee misconduct and to conduct rigorous, in-depth ethics training for FBI Special Agent trainees and others.

A U.S. Navy lieutenant (right) watches as an FBI Special Agent tags the cockpit voice recorder from EgyptAir Flight 990 on the deck of the USS *Grapple* at the crash site. The FBI investigates all airplane crashes where there is the possibility of a criminal act involved in the crash.

USING THE RACKETEER INFLUENCED AND CORRUPT ORGANIZATION (RICO) STATUTE

On October 19, 2004, an expansive racketeering indictment charged 19 members and associates of the New Jersey "Double II" set of the Bloods street gang and their Ohio gun supplier with five murders, 14 attempted murders, seven murder conspiracies, plus numerous aggravated assaults, armed robberies, arson, firearms offenses, and a three-year-long heroin distribution conspiracy.

"We are using the gangs' sophistication against them," said U.S. Attorney General Christopher J. Christie "They have organized themselves into highly structured groups, as the mafia had decades earlier. The same racketeering statutes that brought down the mob will bring down the gangs in northern New Jersey, where they have grown into a frightening, violent menace," said Christie.

The indictment accuses most of the defendants of committing murder or large-scale drug trafficking. Because of that, the usual RICO penalties are enhanced to a maximum of life in prison for those so charged.

In December 2001 a man reported his girlfriend, a young woman, was missing in Anchorage, Alaska. Hikers discovered the severely decomposed remains of a body on Alaska's Seward Highway in June 2002 but the remains were not identified. Finally, in May 2003, her mother submitted a saliva swab sample to the FBI for analysis. The sample was entered in the combined DNA index system for use in the FBI's national missing persons DNA database. The Alaska crime lab and the FBI's nuclear DNA lab got a hit between the mother's nuclear DNA and the remains, showing a possible biological relationship. The FBI lab conducted mtDNA analysis on the remains, compared it to the mother's profile, and found the match. The remains were identified by the coroner, and the case was solved.

The FBI uses various methods to reveal a suspect's fingerprints.

The evidence control unit is responsible for the management and tracking of all evidence from receipt to disposition of the case. Most law enforcement personnel believe physical evidence is more accurate than eyewitness reports, so the evidence must be carefully managed.

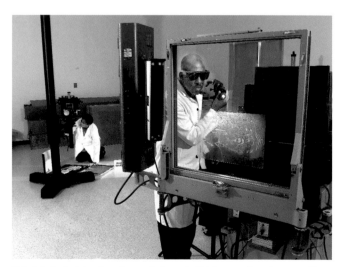

This lab technician is using an "alternate light source" and orange filter goggles to uncover evidence unseen by the naked eye. Tiny particles of body fluids, human hairs, and other organic materials can be revealed by this test.

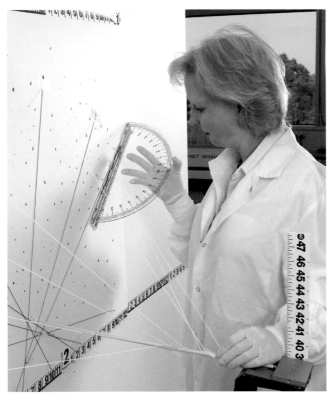

A blood spatter can contain a lot of information. This technician is doing a blood stain pattern interpretation. It involves reconstructing the events that must have happened to produce the bleeding. The technician may take measurements to determine the trajectory and note the way it has been spattered. The way it looks can be useful in determining its origin.

The questioned documents unit in the labs examines and compares data on paper and other evidentiary materials. They have the ability to match torn or perforated edges of items such as paper, stamps, or matches.

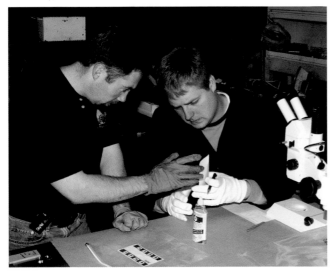

Technicians using adhesive remover are opening one of the suspected letters containing anthrax after it has been decontaminated.

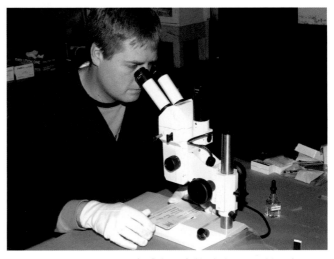

Here a technician is looking for flakes of skin, hair, or anything that would yield DNA.

EVIDENCE RESPONSE TEAM

The FBI's evidence response team (ERT) responds to all federal crime scenes. The ERT is a group of highly trained and specially equipped FBI Special Agents and other personnel who volunteer to conduct major evidence recovery operations.

ERTs collect, identify, manage, and preserve the evidence at crime scenes. They are involved in domestic and international operations, such as the investigation of the bombing of the World Trade Center in 1993, the explosion of Trans-world Airlines (TWA) Flight 800 in 1996, the bombings of two U.S. embassies in East Africa, the bombing of the USS *Cole*, and the terrorist attacks of 9/11.

The ERT consists of Special Agents assigned to a field office's white-collar and governmental fraud squads, foreign counterintelligence squad, drug squad, violent crimes squad, and those conducting background investigations. Support personnel assigned to the team may include the division's photographer and evidence control technicians.

ERT members' initial training consists of an 80-hour program taught by highly experienced FBI forensic instructors. The basic training covers photography, latent fingerprints, crime scene management and documentation, and evidence recovery and packaging. Each of the FBI's 56 field offices' ERT members undergo continuous training to develop and maintain their organizational and forensic skills as new information on forensics develops.

A latent print is a fingerprint that is present and capable of becoming visible, though not now visible. Modern chemistry discovered that cyanoacrylates, like "superglue," make a great unmasker of latent fingerprints. October 2002 saw the Washington, D.C., area hit with a deadly wave of sniper attacks. Local law enforcement took the lead investigation, and the FBI offered its scientific experts to help analyze the evidence. When it was over, a tense three weeks later, 10 people were dead, including an FBI intelligence analyst, and two men were in custody and later convicted of multiple murders. The FBI latent print unit made an unexpected "hit" using the FBI's Integrated Automatic Fingerprint Identification System (IAFIS) that led to the identification and capture of the snipers. More than 400 Special Agents and support personnel served on the case.

Two members of the hazardous materials response team are shown at an exercise in Portland, Oregon, called Red Rose II. This exercise involved a simulated dirty bomb explosion.

On March 15, 1984, the FBI's Greylord investigation into judicial misconduct in Cook County, Illinois, yielded its first conviction, a former deputy traffic court clerk. Other convictions followed. Eighty-two judges, lawyers, clerks, and police officers pled guilty or were convicted in court.

ERTs have been involved in many domestic operations, such as the investigation into the explosion of TWA Flight 800, and in international operations, such as the investigation of U.S. Embassy bombings in East Africa. The team here is surveying and mapping a crime scene.

89

Sacramento emergency response team members are searching for two bodies believed to be buried under a concrete slab. There is no FBI job title "profiler," made famous in the movie *The Silence of the Lambs*. FBI profiling is conducted by teams of Special Agent scientists, engineers, and other disciplines needed to create the profile of a specific criminal. Those involved in profiling look at all aspects of a crime—photographs, interviews, autopsy, laboratory, and investigative reports. What sets profiling apart from other police work is that the conclusions are based on patterns that emerge after comparing the crime scenes of other similar cases and the characteristics of the actual perpetrators in those cases. Some patterns are identified to specific types of individuals. If a body is dumped in a remote area, the killer is probably an outdoors type. If there is no sign of forced entry at the crime scene and evidence that the person lingered, perhaps eating something, then the victim probably knew the killer. With a few elementary facts the FBI agents can begin to draw a profile of the killer: for example, an older male who is probably a hunter or fisherman, who knew the neighborhood, and may be a neighbor. Those clues will help narrow the search down from an almost infinite number of suspects to perhaps a dozen or two.

As of August 2004 the composition of the five categories of profiles of the National DNA Index System (NDIS) was as follows:
Total forensic profiles: 92,284
Total convicted offender profiles: 1,857,140
Total missing persons profiles: 141
Relatives of missing persons profiles: 370
Unidentified human remains profiles: 184
Total number of profiles: 1,950,119

The FBI laboratory's Combined DNA Index System (CODIS) blends forensic science and computer technology into an effective tool for solving violent crimes. CODIS enables federal, state, and local crime labs to exchange and compare DNA profiles electronically, thereby linking crimes to each other and to convicted offenders.

The evidence response team (ERT) uncovered the remains of two males who were believed murdered and buried approximately 12 years ago. The FRT unit has five underwater search teams that are trained in ice, cave, and wreck diving to conduct forensic searches and retrieve evidence. ERTs typically rely on teams of forensic anthropologists, evidence collection specialists, paralegals, photographers, language specialists, and other highly skilled personnel.

The FBI laboratories provide all new Special Agents with six hours of basic and crime scene photography, in addition to surveillance and digital photography.

Special Agents of the evidence response team are recovering human remains at a crime scene. The team must proceed with the recovery as if they are at an archeological dig in order to ensure that no evidence is disturbed before it is documented and photographed.

Modern technology has greatly aided the FBI in victim identification. A technician prepares a bone sample for deoxyribonucleic acid (DNA) analysis. DNA is present in the cells of every living organism. It is most likely found at a crime scene in flakes of skin, hair, semen, or blood. The chances of a person having the same DNA type (except for twins) are one in 100 million. There are two sources of DNA used in forensic analysis. Nuclear DNA (nDNA) is found in blood, saliva, semen, body tissues, and hairs that have tissue at their root ends. Mitochondrial DNA (mtDNA) is typically analyzed in evidence containing naturally shed hairs, bones, and teeth. A technician drills into a bone fragment to attempt to extract mtDNA. Over 1,000 copies of mtDNA can be found in one human cell, whereas there are only two copies of nuclear DNA per cell. The mtDNA can determine ethnicity of the victim. FBI agents must learn how to document, collect, package, and preserve DNA evidence, or it will not be admissible in court.

One of the FBI's longest investigations—17 years—ended in 1996 with the arrest of Theodore Kaczynski, the "Unabomber." His bombs killed three people and injured 23 others. He pleaded guilty and was sentenced to life in prison.

On November 22, 1963, Lee Harvey Oswald assassinated President John F. Kennedy in Dallas, Texas. President Lyndon B. Johnson ordered the FBI to investigate the murder. At that time the FBI had no statutory authority to investigate presidential assassinations.

"All ERT members are on call 24 hours each day," said one member. "We must be prepared to address all types of crime scenes." Following the September 11th attacks in 2001, ERTs searched through mountains of debris at Ground Zero of the World Trade Center, the Fresh Kills landfill on Staten Island, the Pentagon, and the Pennsylvania crash site, looking for clues, identifying human remains, and examining mountains of evidence. They took over 50,000 photographs of the wreckage of the twin towers for possible use as evidence in any future court case.

An ERT typically consists of a team leader and seven to 50 members, all of whom have designated responsibilities, including those of team leader, photographer, sketch preparer, evidence log recorder, evidence custodian, evidence collector/processor, and specialists such as bomb technicians and forensic anthropologists. "It is these skills at a crime scene or at the execution of a search warrant that make the difference in the quality of the evidence that reaches the forensic scientists in the laboratory, and eventually the court," said one agent. "Latent fingerprints, trace evidence, and body fluids yielding DNA are today's valuable evidence." Quality collection and preservation techniques produce good physical evidence, which is critical in the prosecution of a case. "Evidence that has been contaminated, or when the chain of custody has been compromised, is the easiest and most foolish way to lose a case," said one ERT member.

There have been 378,986 potential gun purchases denied by the FBI's National Instant Criminal Background Check System (NICS) section since November 30, 1998. The majority of the denials (333,982) were due to the potential purchasers'/possessors' criminal histories such as felony convictions, domestic violence convictions, or drug abuse. The remaining purchasers were denied for being fugitives from justice, illegal or unlawful aliens, or the subjects of active domestic violence restraining orders.

The following are some of the specialized techniques that the evident response team (ERT) employs:
· Crime scene reconstruction
· Bloodstain pattern analysis
· Gunshot reconstruction and ballistics evidence
· Detection and recovery of human remains and buried body recovery
· Post-blast/bombing crime scene evidence recovery
· Latent fingerprint detection and collection
· Cyanoacrylate fuming for latent prints
· Trace evidence vacuum processing
· Hair and fiber evidence detection and collection
· Electrostatic dust-print lifting
· DNA evidence recovery
· Ground metal detection and ground-penetrating radar
· Casting of shoe and tire impressions and tool-mark evidence
· Evidence collection and packaging
· Crime scene and evidence photography
· Crime scene diagramming and sketching

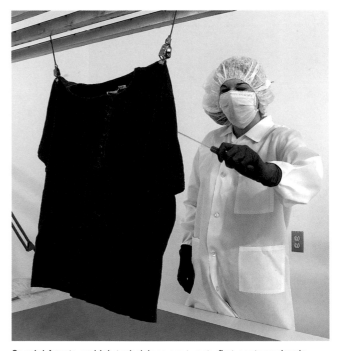

Special Agents and lab technicians are twenty-first-century wizards. With modern technology, they can turn a shard of glass, a flake of dandruff, or a drop of blood into evidence that will lead to the conviction of a murderer, rapist, or serial killer. This forensic science technician is gathering trace evidence that will assist and support a Special Agent's case.

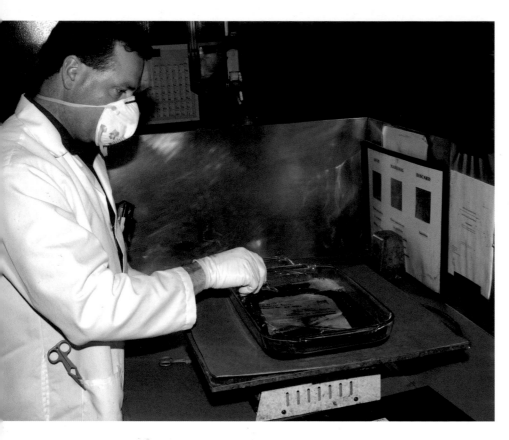

If a chemical, biological, or nuclear threat letter has been found, specially trained FBI agents, local hazardous materials (hazmat) teams, and other first responders are dispatched to the scene. One of the onsite agents immediately contacts FBIHQ counterterrorism, which assembles a multi-agency team for threat assessment/response. The threat letter is sent to a Center for Disease Control-certified lab to make sure it's not contaminated, and it is forwarded to the FBI laboratory in Quantico to test for clues like fingerprints, hair samples, and—if the postage stamp or envelope has been licked—DNA. The letter's language and writing, which could provide important clues, are analyzed by the FBI behavioral science unit.

From the outside, Tom Brokaw's anthrax letter appears virtually identical to a letter received at the *New York Post*. The block handwriting and other characteristics combined to convince the FBI that the letter was probably written and sent by the same person.

A letter found on November 16, 2001, and addressed to Senate Majority Leader Tom Daschle (D-SD), another addressed to Senator Patrick Leahy (D-VT), and other letters were forwarded to experts at the army's Fort Detrick, Maryland, biomedical research laboratory for decontamination to render them safe for forensic analysis in the FBI laboratory.

The successful investigation and prosecution of crimes requires, in most cases, the collection, preservation, and forensic analysis of evidence, which can be crucial to demonstrate guilt or innocence. As one of the largest and most comprehensive forensic laboratories in the world, the FBI laboratory provides forensic and technical services to federal, state, and local law enforcement agencies at no expense to them. The new, state-of-the-art FBI laboratory in Quantico, Virginia, has almost 500,000 square feet of space and a 900-space parking garage. *Henry M. Holden*

Dedicated to the victims of crimes, the new FBI laboratory uses state-of-the-art technology. The FBI laboratory, one of 13 FBI divisions, contains 25 different units. The labs receive more than 600 pieces of evidence a day from law enforcement around the country. *Henry M. Holden*

FOUR

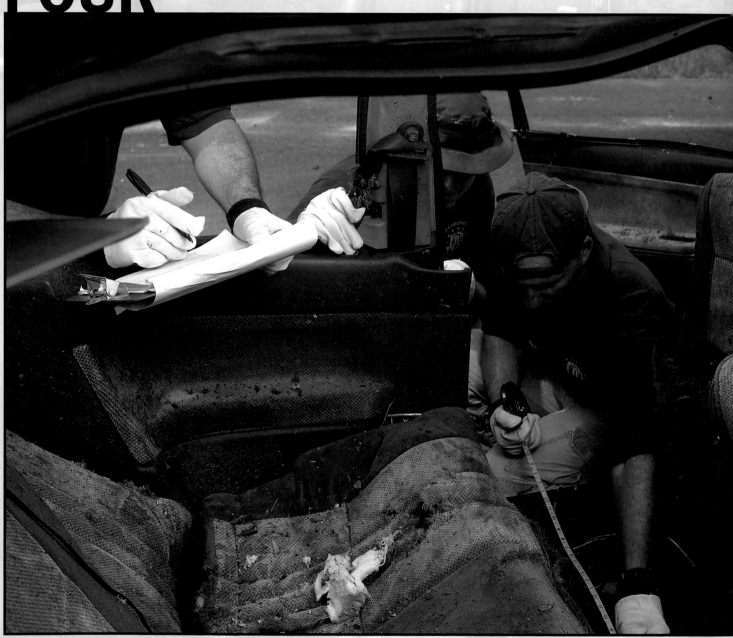

Special Agents and technicians of the explosives unit examine evidence associated with bombings. Explosives examinations involve the identification and function of the components used in the construction of incendiary devices and improvised explosive devices (IED). In addition, the unit performs chemical analyses to determine the type of explosive used in an IED or incendiary device.

The FBI and Terrorism

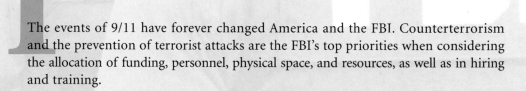

The FBI defines terrorism as the unlawful use of force or violence against persons or property to intimidate or coerce a government, civilian population, or any segment thereof, in furtherance of political or social goals.

The events of 9/11 have forever changed America and the FBI. Counterterrorism and the prevention of terrorist attacks are the FBI's top priorities when considering the allocation of funding, personnel, physical space, and resources, as well as in hiring and training.

DOMESTIC TERRORISM

Since 1908, the FBI has been investigating "homegrown" terrorists. There were incidents in 1919, 1920, 1950, the 1970s, and more in the 1980s. Between 1993 and 1999, the FBI teams of Special Agents, analysts, and other personnel prevented a number of terrorist attacks that could have killed thousands of people. They prevented bombings of federal buildings and halted plots to destroy New York City's critical infrastructure, such as bridges, tunnels, and the FBI field office.

In February 1998, Presidential Decision Directive (PDD) 62 created the National Infrastructure Protection Center (NIPC) and gave the FBI the responsibility for safeguarding the nation's critical infrastructure. This includes computers, telecommunications, banking, electric power, gas and oil systems, water supplies, and government operations.

Today's domestic terror threats represent complex challenges for the FBI. Terrorists are able to operate seamlessly across borders and oceans, aided by sophisticated communications technologies. They finance their operations with elaborate funding schemes, and they patiently and methodically plan their attacks.

While the threat of terrorism is ever present, the FBI has taken significant action in deterring terrorism since the 9/11 terrorist attacks. Under the leadership of Director Robert Mueller, the FBI has moved forward aggressively to implement a comprehensive plan that has one goal in mind: establishing the prevention of terrorism as the Bureau's number one priority. This plan has transformed the FBI, for no longer is the FBI content to concentrate on investigating terrorist crimes after they have occurred, the FBI now is dedicated to disrupting terrorists before they are able to strike. Mueller has overhauled the FBI's counterterrorism operations, expanded its intelligence capabilities, modernized its business practices and technology, and improved coordination with other law enforcement.

Since September 11, 2001, the FBI has disrupted a wide variety of domestic and international terrorist undertakings. During the investigation into the May 12, 2003, bombings in Riyadh, Saudi Arabia, the FBI obtained significant intelligence suggesting the existence of an increased threat of terrorist attacks by the end of summer.

A lab technician from the firearms and tool marks unit is testing a submachine gun that may have been involved in a crime. He will fire several rounds into the water tank, recover the rounds, and then subject them to microscopic examination.

The HMRU provides the capability to safely and effectively respond to criminal acts and incidents involving the use of hazardous materials. They also provide the FBI's technical proficiency and readiness for crime scene and evidence-related operations in cases involving chemical, biological, and radiological materials and wastes. Here the team is demonstrating the containment of an unknown liquid.

Agents and technicians will reconstruct a bomb to determine who or what organization was responsible for it. On the table is a reconstructed pipe bomb attached to an alarm clock timer.

Numerous FBI personnel, including the evidence response team with members of the National Transportation Safety Board (NTSB), had a mountain of wreckage to sift through in the 16-month investigation to determine if the explosion of TWA Flight 800 was an accident or a criminal act. Ninety-six percent of the aircraft was recovered, and there was extensive reconstruction of large sections of the plane. Bomb technicians and laboratory personnel inspected the one-million-plus pieces of aircraft debris. This process included extensive chemical tests and x-rays along with other sophisticated laboratory examinations. *U.S. Coast Guard*

As the many small parts seen in this early photo of the remains of TWA Flight 800 suggest, it was a long and tedious job to reassemble the airliner. The catastrophic explosion just 12 minutes after takeoff of TWA Flight 800 over the Atlantic Ocean near Long Island, New York, on July 17, 1996, resulted in initial speculation that a terrorist attack using a missile or bomb may have been the cause. Just three weeks earlier a bomb had killed 16 Americans in the Khobar Towers in Saudi Arabia. The FBI's joint terrorism task force and the NTSB devoted significant resources to a criminal investigation of the incident. Navy and FBI divers retrieved wreckage weighing more than 60,000 pounds, and the FBI assisted the NTSB in reassembling the aircraft in a hangar to see if it was an act of terrorism. "I had just graduated Quantico," said one agent, "and instead of going to my first field office assignment, I spent ten months helping to put the airplane back together." After a 16-month investigation, the FBI reported the evidence did not point to a criminal or terrorist act. *Department of Defense*

In December 2003, the U.S. intelligence community became concerned about the possibility of near-term attacks in the United States from al Qaeda. Strategic and tactical intelligence pointed to the possibility of attacks during the holiday season and raised concerns about the use of foreign flights, the threats to the energy sector, and the possibility of chemical, biological, or nuclear attacks.

As soon as FBI Headquarters (FBIHQ) received the threat information, it immediately set up a command post in the Strategic Information Operations Center (SIOC) to provide around-the-clock threat analysis and to maintain contact with appropriate joint terrorism task forces (JTTF) and legal attaché (Legat) offices.

Counterterrorism Special Agents and analysts began a full review of all Sunni and Shia international terrorism cases from the past six months to determine if there were any previously unrecognized links. They used the latest software search tools, including link analysis, to ensure that there was no evidence of a connection to any existing terrorism case.

Headquarters directed all 56 of the FBI field offices to take specific actions, including establishing command posts that operated 24 hours a day, seven days a week. These posts gather intelligence through interviews and other means and work with local agencies to increase security, share information, and assist the investigation.

The Iyman Faris case is a good example of how the post-9/11 FBI investigates and attempts to neutralize a specific threat. Faris initially came to the FBI's attention when information from a foreign source linked Faris to terrorists who had plotted attacks to coincide with millennium celebrations. With help from FBI Headquarters, Special Agents and other JTTF members in the Cincinnati, Ohio, field office began an extensive investigation and interviewed Faris in March 2003. During the interview, Faris admitted that he had personal contact with individuals tied to terrorism. At about the same time, another foreign source indicated that an Ohio-based truck driver had been told to attack U.S. bridges—the Brooklyn Bridge in particular. Once that information came together, the Special Agents quickly composed a targeted plan for Faris' interview team, assigned operational leads to field offices and JTTFs around the country, and teamed up with New York police department investigators and analysts.

As a result, Faris was arrested, and he pled guilty to the charge of providing material support or resources to a designated foreign terrorist organization. In October 2003, Faris received a sentence of 20 years in prison. As part of his cooperation agreement with the government, he later provided additional information.

HMRU—Not a Typical Day at the Office

The importance of the FBI's hazardous materials response unit (HMRU) cannot be overstated. A biological attack using the deadly bacteria anthrax had never happened on U.S. soil. Just weeks after the September 11 attacks, five people died of inhalation anthrax. The HMRU members went into high gear. Their job was to recover and analyze the evidence. They were dealing with an invisible killer. "It can be scary work," said one HMRU team member. "But you have to put those feelings behind you and do your job."

Seldom do the HMRU members know exactly what to expect. How hazardous is the material? "We don't always know," said one agent. "As the enemy becomes more sophisticated, the danger becomes more unpredictable and deadly. We have the best equipment for the job, but when I'm heading out there I think that I'd like to see my family one more time, to give them a hug and kiss, and tell them I love them."

The first sign of the anthrax attack came on October 2, 2001, when Robert Stevens, a 63-year-old photo editor, was admitted to a hospital with a high fever. The next day doctors diagnosed Stevens with inhalation anthrax. His death, three days later, was the first reported death from anthrax since 1976.

On October 10, 1995, Amtrak's *Sunset Limited* derailed in the Arizona desert as a result of sabotaged tracks. One Amtrak employee was killed and 78 passengers injured. Two notes, one on each side of the tracks that were signed "Sons of the Gestapo," mentioned the April 1993 federal siege near Waco, Texas, and the shootout in Ruby Ridge, Idaho, in which FBI agents shot and killed the wife and a son of an illegal gun maker in August 1992. The notes were addressed to the Department of Alcohol, Tobacco, and Firearms (ATF), the FBI, state police, and the sheriff's office. No suspects have been arrested in this still-open FBI case.

The coast guard, Immigration and Naturalization Service (INS), FBI, and other agency investigators move into position to open a cargo container suspected of housing Chinese migrants attempting to illegally enter the United States. The container was en route Los Angeles when crewmembers reported hearing tapping emanating from the container. They discovered more than 50,000 pounds of human hair in boxes inside the container. *U.S. Coast Guard*

A day before Stevens went to the hospital, one of National Broadcasting Company (NBC) news anchor Tom Brokaw's assistants and a person who worked with Stevens both came down with symptoms of inhalation anthrax. Letters laced with anthrax spores turned up at the American Broadcasting Company (ABC), the *New York Post*, and in the U.S. Senate mailroom.

One agent recalls, "Initially we had three theories to investigate: the anthrax letters came from al Qaeda, from a domestic terror group, or from a lone individual." With almost 700 Special Agents and lab personnel working on the case, the FBI suspected the spores came from a secret U.S. production process and the letters were the work of an individual.

There were 22 anthrax cases in all; five people died and 17 survived. Currently listed as one of the FBI's top priority investigations, the Amerithrax investigation is an ongoing search for the person or persons responsible for the attacks.

JOINT TERRORISM TASK FORCE

Vital intelligence about terrorists is not produced by the federal government alone. The FBI's more than 12,000 Special Agents are a small cadre compared to the nation's 800,000 state and local law enforcement officers, who are usually the first to encounter and defend against threats. Essential weapons in the battle against terrorism are the 100 joint terrorism task forces (JTTF), which are composed of about 40 agencies and hosted by the FBI. The JTTF represents every major metropolitan area in the United States and is staffed with Special Agents and representatives from federal agencies, state and local law enforcement, and first responders. They often work side-by-side and share information.

The FBI's JTTF program has the primary operational responsibility for terrorism investigations that are not related to ongoing prosecutions. The mission of the national joint terrorism task force (NJTTF) is to enhance communication, coordination, and cooperation by acting as the hub of support for the JTTFs throughout the United States. The NJTTF provides a point of fusion for intelligence acquired in support of counterterrorism operations.

The JTTF has two objectives: to investigate domestic and foreign terrorist groups and individuals targeting or operating within the United States, and to investigate, detect, prevent, and respond to terrorist incidents or terrorist-related criminal activity and prosecute its perpetrators. "What is a real plus-up," said one SAC, "is each agency brings its specific database and its talents to the table. Sharing this type of information can add more pieces to the puzzle. We are constantly trying to connect the dots, and we have made some great leaps in knowledge this way."

The joint terrorism task force (JTTF) began with 11 members from the New York police department and 11 FBI investigators. Prior to September 11, 2001, there were 34 JTTFs in existence.

CRITICAL INCIDENT RESPONSE GROUP

The critical incident response group (CIRG) best illustrates how the FBI Special Agents and their support personnel work as a team. It has approximately 150 Special Agents and 100 professional employees. They work with state, local, federal, and international officials to plan security for high-profile events that might attract terrorists, or coordinate FBI logistics at such events, or respond to crises worldwide when tragedy strikes. The unit works for months in advance with state, local, other federal, and international law enforcement to anticipate what could go wrong, devise prevention strategies, and have alternate plans in place.

Generally, a call comes in from an FBI field office or legal attaché, asking for help with an event or a crisis. A crisis manager makes an assessment and, if needed, may deploy the local FBI SWAT team or an advance team of responders. This group has all the resources of the CIRG behind it, including crisis negotiators, tactical specialists, computer experts, behavioral analysts, and ultimately, the full resources of the FBI.

For example, at the G8 Summit at Sea Island, Georgia, in June 2004, the FBI deployed more than 900 FBI Special Agents and support personnel to help ensure the participants' and the public's safety. Bomb technicians, hostage rescue team members, emergency response team members, and bomb-sniffing dogs were part of the team.

In the case of a full-blown crisis, such as a kidnapping, an aircraft hijacking, a prison escape, the release of a weapon of mass destruction (WMD), and other high-risk violent crimes, the unit immediately dispatches needed personnel and sets up a command post onsite. This is complete with shelter, computers with connections to e-mail and law enforcement databases, fax machines, and office equipment. Depending on where the crisis is, the unit can have a command post up and running in as little as two hours.

A coast guard petty officer searches for terrorists aboard the U.S. Coast Guard Cutter *Neah Bay* during anti-terrorism training with the FBI. *U.S. Coast Guard*

The coast guard and FBI closely work together in maritime operations. *U.S. Coast Guard*

This FBI lab technician is using special software to produce two- and three-dimensional facial reconstruction from skeletal remains, facial age progressions, and postmortem reconstructions.

The FBI, through the NJTTF, identified and interviewed agricultural aircraft owners and operators throughout the country after the 9/11 attacks. The FBI reviewed a list of over 11,000 aircraft provided by the Federal Aviation Administration and interviewed 3,028 crop duster owners and operators of aircraft like this one. This effort has led to several counterterrorism investigations. *Henry M. Holden*

Members of a U.S. Coast Guard law enforcement vessel-boarding team and FBI Special Agents board a vessel from a rigid-hull inflatable (RIB) boat during maritime operations in the Port of Valdez, Alaska, in support of exercise Northern Edge 2002. *Department of Defense*

An FBI Special Agent explosive technician from the Milwaukee, Wisconsin, office displays some of the potentially deadly war souvenirs found at private residences. The FBI promotes public awareness of the danger of collecting war souvenirs. *Department of Defense*

Special Agents have to be prepared to be deployed to any climate and environment. Here a glacier in Alaska dwarfs a Special Agent.

The Anchorage FBI field office deployed a SWAT team to Valdez, Alaska, to work on uncorroborated threats to the Valdez marine terminus.

CRISIS NEGOTIATION UNIT

The crisis negotiation unit (CNU), formed in 1999, is a part of the FBI's CIRG and manages operations, training, research, and program management. As such, the CNU is responsible for the FBI's crisis (hostage) negotiation program.

Crisis negotiation is one the FBI's most effective tools. The successful resolution of thousands of hostage, barricade, attempted suicide, and kidnapping cases throughout the world repeatedly has demonstrated its importance.

The CNU is responsible for the initial training of all FBI Special Agent negotiators, which includes a two-week national crisis negotiation course conducted at the FBI Academy. The unit also provides advanced and periodic update training to Special Agents and other law enforcement negotiators.

In a crisis, the FBI will set up a command center on or near the site of the event.

TRAINING CRISIS NEGOTIATORS

Ideally, direct observation of actual negotiations would be the preferred approach for training and evaluating crisis negotiators. However, the risks to the hostage and the trainee make such an approach impractical, and the infrequency of such events usually does not provide enough opportunities for skill practice. Instead, role playing becomes the next best approach.

Crisis negotiation emphasizes "slowing down" the incident—to expand the timeframe, to allow the subject to vent feelings of anger, frustration, or anxiety, and possibly to defuse the subject's negative emotional state. To accomplish this, the Special Agent negotiators use active listening skills. These have proven critical in establishing a rapport with subjects and calming strong emotions.

ACTIVE LISTENING

Crisis negotiation attempts to soothe the emotions and increase the rationality of the subject. The specific verbal strategies used to accomplish this fall under the category of active listening skills, which are widely considered a negotiator's primary weapon. These skills are critical for the establishment of social relationships in general and the development of rapport between negotiator and subject, particularly in volatile confrontations.

The hostage rescue team (HRT) guarantees a four-hour response to any crisis. The HRT has aircraft prepared and positioned at various strategic locations around the nation to ensure a rapid response. The HRT has an arrangement to use U.S. Air Force aircraft for deployments, like the C-130 Hercules transport plane and tactical helicopters like the MD-530 "little birds." *Henry M. Holden*

All 56 FBI field offices have access to aircraft piloted by FBI agents who have other investigative duties as well. Most aircraft are propeller-driven nonmilitary models, favored for their relatively slow speed and unobtrusive appearance. The FBI has been using airplanes since 1938, when an agent in a Stinson monoplane helped stop an extortion attempt that involved a payoff package thrown from a moving passenger train. The FBI does not do flyovers to listen to telephone calls or gather electronic data from random citizens in hopes the data will provide leads. Rather, the planes are outfitted with electronic surveillance equipment so agents can pursue court-ordered listening devices placed in cars, in buildings, and along streets. Aircraft are now essential in the FBI's domestic war on terror. There was a 60 percent increase in field office requests for airplanes in the year after the 9/11 attacks, with almost 90 percent of air missions now dedicated to surveillance.

Female Special Agents represent 25 percent of the FBI's approximately 400 hostage negotiators.

Some of the active listening skills include:

· Paraphrasing—repeating in one's own words the meaning of the subject's messages;

· Emotion labeling—attaching a tentative label to the feelings expressed or implied by the subject's words or actions;

· Reflecting/mirroring—using statements indicating the ability to take the subject's perspective or repeating last words or main ideas of the subject's message;

· Open-ended questioning—asking questions that stimulate the subject to talk; not eliciting short or one-word answers.

"Training law enforcement personnel in crisis negotiation can be challenging," said one instructor. "Police officers are taught to take charge, to act quickly and with authority. The principles of hostage negotiation fly in the face of that training. A negotiator must fight the inner urge to 'act.' Instead, she [or he] must sit back and use words to diffuse critical, life-and-death situations," he said. To train Special Agent crisis negotiators to resist the urge to act and employ effective listening skills instead takes a considerable amount of time and training. Practice and repetition are crucial.

The best way to predict the students' behavior is to imitate, as closely as possible, the conditions to which they will be exposed in actual crises. Role playing provides the opportunity to practice negotiation skills under safe circumstances designed and manipulated to closely approximate real-world situations.

One set of role-play scenarios—developed by the CNU from incidents requiring a law enforcement response—covers domestic, workplace, and suicide categories. Each scenario includes prearranged prompts delivered by an actor portraying a subject. This helps standardize and extend the length of time of the interactions and make them more similar to real-life encounters.

Early role-play scenarios can last from one to several minutes. Instructors ask students to respond the same way they would if the situation was real. While much shorter than most real-world crisis situations, the format of these brief scenarios allows immediate and frequent instructor feedback. Feedback is especially helpful in the early phases of training, given the importance of the practice and repetition required for new negotiators to gain these skills.

There are longer role plays in Hogan's Alley, where there is a simulated town setting for the training. Scenarios at this level usually last about 40 minutes and allow the negotiators to apply their newly learned skills in an increasingly realistic and stressful situation. For example, negotiators might be asked to respond to a bank robbery gone bad, where the perpetrator is barricaded with hostages. FBI instructors provide the students with a scenario overview, which includes some background on the perpetrator and the setting. Students must make contact with the subject and attempt to resolve the situation peacefully. They will rotate through a series of such scenarios, with team members taking turns in different negotiator roles: primary negotiator, coach, situation board member, intelligence gatherer, team leader, and command post liaison.

A third type of role playing involves the use of longer scenarios, often of several hours. These more realistic role plays reflect actual critical incidents that often require prolonged negotiation periods to be successful. For example, one scenario involves a subject who hijacks a school bus and threatens to blow it up and kill everyone inside if his demands are not met. These role plays require negotiation team members to work together using all of their new skills to resolve the crisis.

The CNU maintains an immediate 24-hour-a-day, seven-day-a-week operational response capability to conduct and manage on-scene negotiations during any crisis event in which the FBI is involved. The CNU is also the negotiation arm of the U.S. government for international incidents. As part of the CNU's operational mission, negotiators are deployed overseas to assist in the management of kidnapping situations involving U.S. citizens. Since 1990, the CNU has aided over 180 such incidents worldwide. The FBI has approximately 340 crisis negotiators in its 56 field offices.

GEORGE BUSH STRATEGIC INFORMATION OPERATIONS CENTER (SIOC)

The George Bush Strategic Information Operations Center (SIOC)—located on the fifth floor of the J. Edgar Hoover FBI Building in Washington, D.C.—serves as the FBI's 24-hour clearinghouse for strategic information and the center for crisis management and special-event monitoring. It supports major case investigations, tactical operations, and exercises.

The heightened need for timely information prompted FBIHQ to re-evaluate the suitability of the existing 4,000-square-foot operations center in the mid 1990s. The SIOC's increasing involvement in special events and large-scale and sometimes multiple crises, has expanded the role of the FBI and made it a lead agency in joint investigations.

In the Strategic Information and Operations Center (SIOC), personnel must have a top-secret sensitive compartmentalized information (SCI) security clearance to enter the center unescorted, and a sign at the reception desk reiterates this. Everyone who enters SIOC must check all cell phones, pagers, and other electronic devices at the reception desk.

The new SIOC—with 40,000 square feet of offices and operations and technical support areas—has secure communications, computer links, and video conferencing. The center is shielded to prevent electronic signals from entering or leaving the facility. Within the SIOC are four 2,500-square-foot operations areas, five smaller crisis action team (CAT) rooms, with 16 adjacent breakout rooms designed to handle multiple major events and/or smaller operations simultaneously. Room configurations can be changed, widened, or partitioned to meet the center's specific requirements.

In times of crisis, teams form in the SIOC, complementing the 24-hour day-to-day watch team. These CATs focus solely on a particular investigation, serving as a headquarters-level clearinghouse and distribution site for information. In large-scale investigations where multiple field offices are involved, the CAT acts as a centralized command post, albeit remote from a particular crisis.

In the SIOC's executive conference room, two 50-inch flat-screen TVs rise at the touch of a button from built-in floor cabinets. Digital clocks line the wall, displaying time in countries around the world, and 60 miles of fiber optic cable run under the floor. Recessed outlets in the conference table pop up to allow access to classified and unclassified computer systems. These outlets also permit laptop computers to interface with the presentation system to display their information onto the flat-screen TVs or a drop-down screen mounted into the ceiling, and to connect telephones for secure and non-secure conference calls. Overhead cameras with zoom capabilities

Attorney General Janet Reno and former President George H. W. Bush at the dedication of the Strategic Information and Operations Center (SIOC) at FBI Headquarters in November 1998.

Bomb data center specialists develop techniques, technology, and equipment that minimizes the hazards associated with bomb disposal, and administer the training for the FBI's special agent bomb technician program. A bomb technician operates the Andros Mark 5 A1 state-of-the-art robotic device used to safely disarm a bomb.

SECURITY CLEARANCE

All FBI Special Agents have a top-secret clearance. This clearance is applied when the unauthorized disclosure of information or material could reasonably be expected to cause exceptionally *grave damage* to national security. In addition, some classified information is so sensitive that even the extra protection measures applied to top-secret information are not sufficient. This information is known as "sensitive compartmented information" (SCI). To have access to classified information, one must possess two necessary elements: a level of security clearance at least equal to the classification of the information, and the need to know the information in order to perform one's duties.

This display in the Strategic Information and Operations Center (SIOC) shows the exact portions of the earth that are in daylight and those that are in darkness (in real time). As the seasons change, the light pattern will reflect this throughout a year. In the lower left, the days of the week are observed on either side of the International Dateline. The display actually moves as you watch. This display is approximately 35 inches by 23 inches.

A hostage rescue team will use handguns, rifles, and submachine guns. They will wear fire-retardant Nomex hoods, goggles, flame-retardant jumpsuits, bulletproof body armor, multi-pocketed tactical vests fitted for ammunition magazines, first aid kits, and various grenades. They may also wear night-vision goggles and use padded ladders (to minimize noise), linear explosives, distraction devices (such as flash-bang grenades), chemical munitions (tear gas), body armor, microphones, video systems, battering rams, sledgehammers, gas masks, and bolt cutters.

The HRT's Latin motto is *Servare Vitas*, To Save Lives. HRT operators are discouraged from firing their weapons unless it is absolutely necessary; but they go in prepared. They train using real bullets and real explosives, and there is real danger in the training. The training is redundant. It is meant to be so that in a combat situation, the tactics will be second nature.
Department of Defense

All hostage rescue team (HRT) operators serve a one-year probation period. The average operator has about eight years of experience as a Special Agent and is in his late 30s. He may be married with children. Less than half of HRT operators have prior military experience. There is a three-year minimum commitment to the team, and most operators serve five to seven years before moving on to another FBI special agent job. *Department of Defense*

allow documents to be displayed on the TVs or the drop-down screen. Showers, sleeping quarters, and cooking facilities are available in the building in case of a prolonged crisis.

A TYPICAL DAY AT NJTTF

On a "typical day" there may be about 60 people from 40 U.S. agencies—law enforcement, intelligence, diplomacy, defense, public safety, and homeland security—on site. The SIOC is essentially a one-stop shopping center for intelligence on terrorism.

"It's a pretty simple concept," said one senior agent. "We bring together people from every U.S. agency that collects and processes terrorist intelligence. We put them in one room and hook them into their own and into our intelligence databases, and suddenly, we have the universe of terrorist intelligence on the table—to share, to query, to coordinate, to answer questions, and to give direction and support to the JTTFs around the country that function under us. The terrorist intelligence is instantly shared vertically from HQ to our JTTFs and horizontally to all the national JTTF agencies."

A normal day in SIOC begins at 5 a.m. "We have an informal meeting and collate the day's hot issues from our multiple sources, and circulate them to everyone to digest, process, and query," said a senior agent. "At 8 a.m., there's a small coordination meeting with the CT [counterterrorism] watch and SIOC supervisors on the day's briefings. Then, at 9:30 a.m. sharp, everyone in the room turns off their computers, telephones, everything, and we hold an intense, formatted briefing. We cover all the top and breaking issues. We solicit input from everyone in the room for breaking news from his or her agency. We get a detailed briefing from the CT watch on the current threat stream. We field questions and talk strategies and logistics. Then we get to work, and that can mean many things. People send items of interest to their home agencies and run down the answers to questions their agencies have asked. They query their agency's databases to answer thousands of lead and name check questions from the JTTFs. They coordinate special terrorism projects and, if necessary, unleash all 100 JTTFs to address an issue, fill in an intelligence gap, solve a problem, or activate just one to address a local threat. Every day is pretty intense."

If an incident or an attack occurs in the United States, local police are usually the first to respond. If, in their judgment, the situation requires a larger response or the crime is federal in nature, they call the FBI for assistance or to take the lead in the case. The FBI has a SWAT team in each of the 56 field offices nationwide, and there are nine enhanced SWAT teams of about 30 agents each in large field offices such as New York, Chicago, Washington, D.C., and Los Angeles. These teams have special training from the FBI hostage rescue team (HRT) operators and additional enhanced equipment. Their job is to neutralize the threat or, if they cannot, control the situation until the HRT arrives.

The senior agent continued, "There are a lot of possible threats on the table right now. To identify potential terrorist sleeper cells, Operation Tripwire commissions all JTTFs to ask specific questions of specific industries (e.g., suspicious behavior of airline passengers, or [at] a nuclear power plant). Then we look for patterns from the collected data. We're collecting and analyzing data on radicalism in prisons, and we're coordinating new initiatives for railroads and cruise ships.

"We are also coordinating through the terrorism threat task force, new iterations of Operation Tripwire—this time having our JTTFs collect data on ferry systems and on the sale of unmanned aerial vehicles. These kinds of projects really show the heart of the national JTTF mission. When all our agencies work together as we do, we can find better ways to help disrupt, dismantle, and eliminate terrorist threats."

HOSTAGE RESCUE TEAM— *SERVARE VITAS*—"TO SAVE LIVES"

The FBI's hostage rescue team (HRT) is a special counterterrorist unit tasked with responding to terrorist incidents within the United States. The HRT is also responsible for the capture and return of federal fugitives from abroad.

The FBI has had great success over the years dealing with criminals, but in the past, some hostages died in attempts to free them from hostage situations. One Special Agent, Danny O. Coulson, believed the FBI needed a specially trained squad dedicated to saving hostages' lives. The need for a unit like this was first recognized in the late 1970s as worldwide terrorism increased. Coulson had dealt with terrorists and other criminals, and later became the first commander of the Bureau's hostage rescue team in 1983.

This is the aircraft accident crash site where U.S. Senator Paul Wellstone died on October 25, 2002, when his plane crashed on Minnesota's Iron Range. All eight people aboard the plane died. The FBI sent a 15-person evidence recovery team to the crash site. "When there is a U.S. senator on board, we take all the precautions to make sure this was just an accident," said Paul McCabe, an FBI Special Agent who works in Minneapolis. The later investigation revealed pilot error that caused the crash.

The HRT offers a tactical option to a hostage situation. In a way, it is a "special forces" unit that is somewhat similar to a military force. However, the members of HRT are not soldiers or commandos, but FBI Special Agents who can make arrests and testify in court. Unlike the military special forces, HRT operators are trained to understand the legal implications of their actions. They must operate within the Constitution of the United States, and are accountable for all their actions, including every round fired in a situation. The Office of Professional Responsibility serves to judge the HRT or the individual operator's actions.

The HRT is the last resort for civilian law enforcement and is never used as a first strike option. When attempting to resolve a crisis, the FBI will use every other means available before calling in the HRT.

Hostage taking generally involves terrorists using weapons, making every situation more dangerous. This presents a challenge for HRT operators. They need patience, careful planning, and courage to face an unknown weapons threat, while neutralizing the terrorists, yet also keeping the hostages alive. This requires critical and careful selection of team members, and intensive training is imperative.

HRT operators must be in superb physical condition. They will have to climb ropes, swim, run, crawl through narrow spaces, parachute, rappel down ropes from cliffs, and fast-rope down from helicopters. *Department of Defense*

A Special Agent is setting up a bullet to examine under a microscope. In July 1992, the FBI laboratory installed DrugFire, a database that stores and links specific, unique markings left on bullets and shell casings after a gun is fired. Facts on spent ammunition recovered at drug-related shootings are stored in DrugFire and used to link crimes committed with the same gun.

Taking hostages goes back hundreds of years. One of the most famous cases was England's King Richard I, "The Lionhearted." Richard insulted Duke Leopold of Austria, and Leopold had him kidnapped in 1192 and held him for ransom. It took England two years to raise the $67,000 to free him.

HRT TRAINEE SELECTION

Selecting the right people for the HRT is a grave responsibility, as it is the last line of defense in civilian law enforcement. While HRT operators have one of the most challenging and exciting jobs in the FBI, to become an operator is to go through a grueling, Darwinian process that only the strongest and fittest can survive.

Assignment to the HRT is voluntary and open to all qualified Special Agents of the FBI. HRT candidates are selected based on their background and experience, but only those who display exceptional physical and mental performance during a rigorous two-week selection course will make the cut. Even then, this only demonstrates they are worthy of consideration for training as an HRT operator. Often candidates will spend months before the selection tests honing their physical conditioning and shooting skills. Any Special Agent can apply for HRT as long as they have at least three years of field experience and a "superior" performance appraisal. Over the years, three women have applied for the HRT, but to date none have made it through the trainee selection process. This is not due to discriminatory practices, but for only one factor involved in HRT operator-trainee selection: performance (not age, sex, or size). If agents make the cut, they become part of the team. If not, they will return to another satisfying career within the Bureau.

The HRT trainee selection process is a major challenge for those prepared, and it shows no mercy to the unprepared. Unlike other FBI special agent training, this one is designed to make candidates fail. The FBI cannot afford to have operators fail in a real tactical situation. All candidates will have to reach deep inside themselves for the strength to make it, but not all will not be able to reach deeply enough.

On November 12, 2001, American Airlines Flight 587 crashed in Queens, New York. At the time, the FBI had most of its agents working on the World Trade Center and Pentagon terrorist attacks that happened two months earlier. Still, it had to allocate personnel to determine if, as some speculated, it was a terrorist attack. It was later determined that the cause of the crash was pilot error and an aircraft structural failure not attributed to a criminal act. *U.S. Coast Guard*

The trainee selection process and HRT training are obscured in secrecy, but all the trainee candidates are FBI Special Agents who will do their homework. Some will call friends, and others will talk with agents who gave their best but missed the opportunity to become part of the HRT. Still, those who have not made the cut cannot adequately prepare the candidates for what is ahead of them.

Trainee candidates are allowed no jewelry or watches and wear only the issued uniforms, which consist of an alphanumeric-labeled vest over a blue T-shirt and blue shorts (or camouflage depending on the exercise), and a wristband. The alphanumeric designation is designed to keep a certain amount of anonymity. "The uniforms remove the person's individuality and prepare them to begin to identify with the team," said one agent.

On the first day, trainee candidates will undergo a grueling test of their physical conditioning, beginning with a 110-yard shuttle run from the prone position, a 2.5-mile run, climbing 20-foot ropes, and doing a minimum of 50 pushups and 12 pull-ups, among other tests. In order to stay competitive, candidates must at least double these numbers. The unprepared will drop out on the first day. The instructors, who are all HRT operators, will watch for looks of anxiety on the faces of the candidates. They will be looking for character short-comings that affect the way the candidate performs under pressure. If the candidates exhibit any of these or other negative emotional behaviors, these factors will be taken into account during the selection process. Only the fittest will survive. The HRT wants only individuals who show no fear or self-doubt and who are highly competitive.

An FBI Special Agent takes a report at a joint tactical operations center set up to deal with the aftermath of a hurricane. *Department of Defense*

FBI fingerprint experts look over supplies in a temporary mortuary/identification center set up to identify the remains of aircraft crash victims. *Department of Defense*

This bomb blast training exercise is called the "powder train." It is a demonstration of how quickly low explosives burn, what color smoke each powder puts out, and what sort of residue is left over. It starts with the improvised low explosive called potassium chlorate/sugar then goes to single base smokeless powder, double base smokeless powder, pyrodex, Fg black powder (BP), FFg BP, FFFg BP, and then ends up with FFFFg BP. The potassium chlorate/sugar mixture started out slow with lots of white smoke, and it burned down the line. It ended up going very fast when it hit the pyrodex and black powder at the end.

Another bomb blast training exercise is called "pillars of fire," named after the three jugs of gasoline on the ground. Each had a length of detonation (det) cord inside. Each length of det cord was attached to a main line, which ran the width of the range. They were then initiated from left to right. The det cord detonated and the gas fumes ignited, creating fire columns that were very loud and very hot.

Most exercises in the training curriculum are taken from actual HRT operations. One of the open-ended tests is the "dog run," named after an incident where an escaped kidnapper led authorities on a three-week chase through the Grand Canyon. Trainee candidates track a suspect across rough terrain and through creeks and gullies in Quantico for miles. The number of miles is a closely guarded secret to impose physical and mental anxiety, since the trainees never know how far they will have to go before the exercise is over.

After the physical tests comes the psychological test. The Minnesota multiphasic personality inventory (MMPI) is designed to assess major symptoms of social and personal maladjustment, and also identify emotionally stable individuals for high-risk, high-stress public safety positions such as law enforcers, firefighters, and nuclear power facilities personnel—individuals who are more likely to reinforce the safety of others.

Trainee candidates are also tested for aquaphobia (an irrational fear of water) and acrophobia (the abnormal dread of great heights). The HRT has to be ready for anything, anywhere, and in a tactical operation, agents may have to rescue hostages from a boat, which may require swimming long distances. The aquaphobia test is designed so only the most fearless swimmers will pass. In one timed test, the trainee candidates have to swim through frigid water (indoors). In another, blindfolded trainees must walk 75 feet under water, carrying a 30-pound weight in their hands. If they surface before finishing their "walk," they fail.

The agoraphobia test is also one of confidence, and it is dangerous. One test involves the trainee candidates climbing a completely vertical 50-foot ladder, and another where the individuals have to crawl up the outside of a four-story building. They have been told before the test that there are no nets, and if they fall, they will fail and probably die. They have two choices: climb or do not. Those who choose not to climb, fail.

At times, the operators will use hunger to analyze the trainee candidates' behavior and force them to share a single meal among two or three people. The instructors will look for greed, anger, or other negative character flaws. "If we see any, they're out. We want only people who can work together and look out for each other as a team," said one instructor.

At other times, the operators will use fatigue to test the mental stamina of the individuals. To train HRT members to function under great fatigue, they are exercised to the point of exhaustion and then given decision-making problems. Often the trainee candidates are also suffering from sleep deprivation. They may practice for hours in rain, snow, or amidst woods filled with biting and sucking insects and high humidity. The reality is, an HRT mission may last several days in a hostile environment, and sleep in these situations is not an option.

All current HRT operators are an integral part of the selection process. They go through the same course, eating the same dirt, sweating with the candidates, and running the same obstacles as they do. This gives the operators a close-up opportunity to take copious notes on each candidate's performance. Their lives will depend on who they select.

HRT training is more than physical skills and shooting ability. It is about the willingness to help a fellow operator in a life-and-death situation. In a real situation an HRT operator may have to carry a wounded fellow operator or hostage to safety. In preparation for such a situation, part of this course includes carrying a fellow trainee candidate 60 yards. If the candidate cannot carry the weight in a real-life situation, both operators may die. That would jeopardize the safety of the mission, and it is all about the safety of the team and the mission. Before the selection process is over, the trainee candidates will run on the infamous "yellow brick road."

YELLOW BRICK ROAD

The yellow brick road is the ultimate challenge for the HRT trainee candidates. They have all gone through the yellow brick road as NATs, but this time it is different. Trainee candidates must run a longer, 12-mile yellow brick road wearing a military flak jacket, two canteens of water, and a long weapon such as an M14.

Next comes the 15-foot cargo net. After flipping over the top of the net, most trainee candidates will have to pause to catch their breath before continuing the last 3/4 mile, which includes a combat crawl through muddy water and under barbed wire to the finish line. The trainee candidates who finish will have survived a unique physical challenge and, in the process, learned some valuable lessons about themselves.

HRT never discloses how many slots it will fill, but on average, about 1/3 of the trainee candidates will make it through the two-week selection process. However, HRT may not need all those chosen, so only the best among them will continue HRT training. Once selected, prospective members undergo a four-month, highly secret training program in new operator training school (NOTS).

HRT operators train for the worst-case scenario, knowing that when they are deployed by the director, it will be because something, somewhere, has gone terribly wrong, and they are the last resort to maintaining the rule of law. They know it will not be a cakewalk, and they will be putting their lives on the line.

Federal law prohibits military action in domestic affairs without a specific presidential order. Military antiterrorist groups like the Delta force and navy SEALs are prohibited by federal law from performing civilian law enforcement duties in the United States or its possessions. *Posse Comitatus* (meaning "power or force of the country" in Latin) is derived from ancient English law enforcement, which consisted of the shire's force of able-bodied private citizens summoned to assist in maintaining public order.

FIVE

A bomb squad technician is sampling the air around a bomb, looking for clues to the type of bomb it is. The components of a bomb have distinct chemical signatures, and knowing what is inside may dictate how to disarm the device.

A Global FBI

The laboratory's explosives unit and evidence response team unit traveled to Saudi Arabia to investigate the Khobar Towers crime scene. FBI personnel—working in 120-degree temperatures—sifted through tons of debris, removing human remains and collecting bombing vehicle parts, weapons, and ammunition from the scene.

The FBI is very successful at building both criminal and intelligence cases with information based on detailed investigations in which the facts are substantiated. Hunting down global terrorists has presented new challenges to the FBI.

The FBI has implemented training programs that focus on the skills and knowledge necessary for counterterrorism and counterintelligence investigations and intelligence functions. "We give all new agents 110 hours of counterterrorist and counterintelligence training," said one senior agent. "We reworked the traditionally law enforcement-focused program to emphasize how intelligence and criminal investigative techniques are used in tandem as part of the FBI's strategic mission. We are emphasizing development of an intelligence base through the operation of human sources and liaison with other agencies."

The FBI works with other federal law enforcement agencies to guard the United States borders from terrorist incursions. The Immigration and Customs Enforcement Agency (ICE, formally known as U.S. Customs) monitors the southern border of the United States from its Riverside, California, base. *Immigration and Customs Enforcement Agency*

Prior to September 11, 2001, the FBI produced very few raw intelligence reports; its primary mission was to investigate and prosecute criminal activities. Therefore, the FBI did not produce a significant number of counterterrorism-related intelligence information reports. Following the 9/11 terrorist attacks, the FBI's primary mission changed to protecting the United States from terrorist attacks. For the past three years, the FBI has transformed itself into an organization that is actively investigating and disrupting terrorist operations. As part of that transformation, the FBI has developed a strong intelligence program that is responsible for intelligence gathering and analysis, which includes the production of intelligence information reports. The increase in the number of these reports produced by the FBI after 9/11 reflects the change in the FBI's primary mission and is a result of the formation of an intelligence program within the FBI. In 2003, there were 2,109 intelligence information reports containing raw intelligence derived from counterterrorism-related FBI investigations and intelligence collection.

Prior to September 11, the Bureau also had no centralized structure for the management of its counterterrorism program. Terrorism cases were routinely managed out of individual field offices. An al Qaeda case, for example, might have been run out of the New York field office; a Hamas case might have been managed by the Washington, D.C. field office. As a result, only a few of the larger field offices, and a handful of analysts at FBIHQ and at the Counter Terrorism Center (CTC), possessed the majority of the institutional knowledge about al Qaeda and the threat it posed to the United States.

However, the FBI has a history of successfully conducting counterterrorism investigations through to prosecution. From the apprehension of Theodore Kaczynski, a.k.a, the "Unabomber," to the investigation and prosecution of those responsible for the 1993 World Trade Center bombing, the 1995 Oklahoma City bombing, and the 1998 bombings of two U.S. embassies in East Africa, the FBI has investigated terrorist acts and helped to bring many of those responsible to justice.

EMBASSY BOMBINGS

On August 7, 1998, a bomb exploded near the U.S. Embassy in Nairobi, Kenya. The bomb killed 212 people, including 12 Americans and 31 foreign service nationals employed at the embassy. Another 4,735 people were wounded in the terrorist attack. The bombing of the U.S. Embassy in Tanzania, on the same day, killed 11 people, including seven foreign service nationals. Another 72 people, including two Americans, were wounded in the terrorist attack. The FBI immediately deployed agents to East Africa to assist in the search, rescue, and investigative efforts. The investigation of the crime scenes, in cooperation with the host countries, included over 1,000 interviews. At the time, this investigation was the largest overseas deployment of personnel in FBI history. The FBI named the investigation in Tanzania "tanbom," combining the words Tanzania and bombing.

(Right) The amount of factual and corroborated information developed by FBI Special Agents led to a sealed indictment against Osama bin Laden in federal court. On June 7, 1999, the FBI placed Bin Laden on the "10 most wanted" list for his alleged involvement in the bombing of the two embassies in Africa. Quick work by the FBI and other teams dedicated to tracking Bin Laden and his network linked two dozen suspects to Bin Laden. Four individuals were arrested, and on May 29, 2001, the U.S. Attorney's Office and the FBI announced the convictions of the four menin connection with the bombings. The four individuals were sentenced to life in federal prison without the possibility of release. The investigation continues because several suspects remain as fugitives.

The FBI recorded eight terrorist incidents and one prevention of a planned terrorist attack in the United States and its territories in 2000. Domestic terrorists perpetrated each of the eight terrorist incidents. Special-interest terrorists, specifically animal rights and environmental extremists, carried out the attacks.

FBI TEN MOST WANTED FUGITIVE

**MURDER OF U.S. NATIONALS OUTSIDE THE UNITED STATES;
CONSPIRACY TO MURDER U.S. NATIONALS OUTSIDE THE UNITED STATES;
ATTACK ON A FEDERAL FACILITY RESULTING IN DEATH**

USAMA BIN LADEN

Date of Photograph Unknown

Aliases: Usama Bin Muhammad Bin Ladin, Shaykh Usama Bin Ladin, the Prince, the Emir, Abu Abdallah, Mujahid Shaykh, Hajj, the Director

DESCRIPTION

Date of Birth:	1957	**Hair:**	Brown
Place of Birth:	Saudi Arabia	**Eyes:**	Brown
Height:	6' 4" to 6' 6"	**Complexion:**	Olive
Weight:	Approximately 160 pounds	**Sex:**	Male
Build:	Thin	**Nationality:**	Saudi Arabian
Occupation:	Unknown		
Remarks:	Bin Laden is the leader of a terrorist organization known as Al-Qaeda, "The Base." He is left-handed and walks with a cane.		

CAUTION

**USAMA BIN LADEN IS WANTED IN CONNECTION WITH THE AUGUST 7, 1998, BOMBINGS OF
THE UNITED STATES EMBASSIES IN DAR ES SALAAM, TANZANIA, AND NAIROBI, KENYA.
THESE ATTACKS KILLED OVER 200 PEOPLE. IN ADDITION, BIN LADEN IS A SUSPECT IN
OTHER TERRORIST ATTACKS THROUGHOUT THE WORLD.**

CONSIDERED ARMED AND EXTREMELY DANGEROUS

**IF YOU HAVE ANY INFORMATION CONCERNING THIS PERSON, PLEASE CONTACT YOUR
LOCAL FBI OFFICE OR THE NEAREST U.S. EMBASSY OR CONSULATE.**

REWARD

The Rewards For Justice Program, United States Department of State, is offering a reward of up to $25 million for information leading directly to the apprehension or conviction of Usama Bin Laden. An additional $2 million is being offered through a program developed and funded by the Airline Pilots Association and the Air Transport Association.

www.fbi.gov

Hostage rescue team (HRT) operators are trained to handle any incident in any environment.

Hostage rescue team (HRT) operators may sometimes use explosives to breech a door.

Beginning in 1985, the FBI began investigating violations of the Hostage Taking Statute, and in 1986 the Overseas Homicide/Attempted Homicide Statute went into law. Due to these statutes, FBI Special Agents could, for the first time, actively and aggressively respond to major terrorist incidents abroad where American citizens and property were the victims. The FBI's role as a lead agency in terrorism matters is further supported by presidential decision directive (PDD) 39 and PDD 62. PDD 39 sets forth the United States counterterrorism policy and outlines the FBI's jurisdictional responsibilities in relation to terrorism. PDD 39 also grants the Department of Justice—acting through the FBI—responsibility for leading the operational response to a weapons of mass destruction incident.

The U.S. Congress has five primary committees that regularly oversee all aspects of FBI operations:

· The House/Senate Judiciary Committees
· The House/Senate Intelligence Committees
· The House/Senate Appropriations Committees
· The House Government Reform Committee
· The Senate Governmental Affairs Committee

Beyond the role played by the U.S. Congress, FBI operations are also observed by the director of central intelligence (and in the future, the new director of national intelligence), the Department of Justice Office of Intelligence Policy and Review, and the Intelligence Oversight Board, appointed from members of the President's Foreign Intelligence Advisory Board.

Hostage rescue team (HRT) operators must be fearless of heights.

Hostage rescue team (HRT) operators may travel overseas on a rendition to capture and return fugitives to America. To date, no FBI Special Agent has died on a rendition.

KEY FEDERAL LAWS THAT APPLY TO FBI INVESTIGATIONS AND OPERATIONS:

- The U.S. Constitution
- The Foreign Intelligence Surveillance Act of 1978
- The 1968 Federal Wiretap Statute (Title III), as amended
- The Civil Rights Act of 1967
- The Privacy Act of 1974
- The Whistleblower Protection Act of 1989, Intelligence Community Whistleblower Protection Act of 1998, and various government and FBI provisions and regulations
- The Freedom of Information Act of 1966

The FBI participated in preventing many terrorist acts before 9/11, such as the foiling of the "millennium plot" to plant explosives at Los Angeles International Airport, the apprehension and prosecution of Ramzi Yousef and others for conspiracy to bomb U.S. commercial airliners, and the arrest and prosecution of Sheik Omar Abdel Rahman and his co-conspirators before they could carry out their plan to bomb office buildings, bridges, and tunnels in New York City.

A good example of the FBI's ability to exploit and share evidence for its intelligence value is the use of the al Qaeda terrorism handbook seized from an al Qaeda location overseas. The intelligence gleaned from the handbook provided useful guidance about al Qaeda's interests and capabilities.

FBI AND AL QAEDA

Through operational and intelligence sources, the FBI identified the first seeds of an Islamic terrorism campaign in the United States in 1989. They used all the intelligence and investigative techniques available to identify potential terrorist subjects, and attempt to determine their objectives. Photographs taken during some of these investigations became important later when individuals were recently identified as subjects in early terrorism cases. An individual photographed at a shooting range in the late 1980s was later convicted in the 1990 murder of Meir Kahane, head of the Jewish Defense League, and was also convicted for his involvement in the World Trade Center bombing in 1993 and for planning to bomb various New York City landmarks.

It was through these early investigations that the name Osama bin Laden first surfaced, initially as an organizer and financier of military training camps in Afghanistan, and later connected to the 1993 World Trade Center Bombing and the foiled New York City infrastructure attacks. The FBI opened an intelligence investigation into Bin Laden in February 1996; a criminal investigation began in September. "One of the most significant factors in the progress of the investigations, from the FBI perspective," said one senior agent, "came with the arrival of an al Qaeda defector, Jamal Al Fadl, nicknamed 'Junior.'"

"Junior had offered his information to a number of different countries before being brought in by the CIA [Central Intelligence Agency]," the agent said. "Later, the CIA allowed Junior to meet with the FBI, and Junior became an FBI cooperating witness against al Qaeda. Information provided by Junior spurred a continuing effort to target and apprehend al Qaeda associates, including those willing to act as informants."

The FBI learned that al Qaeda operatives studied American military manuals, that al Qaeda set up its own internal security system, and that its operatives are selected, in part, on their ability to assimilate into other societies and cultures. "We also learned that al Qaeda operatives continue to travel to other countries to marry into local society and set up front companies."

Junior was only one of several informants for the FBI. Like Junior, informants continue to provide the FBI with new information. "Through these informants, we have gained valuable information into al Qaeda's leadership, organization, methods, training, finances, geographical reach, and intent. Much of this information is passed on to the military."

Federal law enforcement efforts received a significant boost with the passage of the Antiterrorism and Effective Death Penalty Act of 1996. This law, signed by President Clinton in April 1996, includes new measures aimed at countering both domestic and international terrorism. Section 302 of this act directs the secretary of state, in conjunction with the U.S. attorney general and the secretary of the treasury, to designate any organization that meets certain proscribed criteria as a foreign terrorist organization (FTO). To qualify for this designation, an organization must be a foreign organization and engage in terrorist activities that threaten the security of United States nationals or the national security of the United States.

WORLD TRADE CENTER BOMBING

For terrorists, car bombs are one weapon of choice. They are relatively simple and inexpensive to make, they can be enormously destructive, and they can have a serious negative psychological impact on a population.

On February 26, 1993, a bomb exploded in the World Trade Center's underground garage, leaving a 100-foot-wide, four-story-deep crater. It killed six people and injured over 1,000 others. The JTTF, an FBI-led task force that includes FBI and other federal agencies, worked on the investigation with the New York City and New York/New Jersey port authority police.

The blast was so powerful that it destabilized the area around the site of the explosion, which delayed the intensive examination of the bombed site that is usually necessary to yield important clues. There were hundreds of vehicles buried beneath tons of concrete and steel. Determining who was responsible would be like putting together a giant jigsaw puzzle made of many tiny parts.

Plastic explosives destroy a car during a demonstration. *Department of Defense*

Hostage rescue team (HRT) operators train in a simulated airline hijacking.

CRITICAL ELEMENTS: INTELLIGENCE

Special Agents are currently evaluated according to specified performance criteria related to "critical elements." These elements provide guidance and define the activities the FBI expects the agents to undertake and master. In March 2004, the FBI revised the evaluation criteria for all Special Agents to emphasize intelligence objectives to include critical element seven (intelligence collection and reporting), which requires each Special Agent to demonstrate and effectively apply knowledge, authority, and the mandates governing intelligence functions. Critical element eight (developing an intelligence base) measures how Special Agents effectively cultivate and exploit intelligence sources.

SPECIAL AGENT CAREER TRACKS

Traditionally, the Bureau has recruited, trained, rewarded, and promoted its agents primarily for law enforcement work. This approach is no longer adequate now that intelligence work has assumed such a central role in the efforts to prevent terrorism. In March 2004, the FBI established a new career path for Special Agents designed with three objectives. First, the career path will give all agents experience with intelligence and analysis. Second, it will give agents an opportunity to develop specialized skills, experience, and aptitudes in one of the four program areas: intelligence, counterterrorism/counterintelligence, cyber, or criminal. Third, it will make intelligence expertise and experience a prerequisite for promotion to senior supervisory ranks.

The FBI uses the most sophisticated communications equipment available.

FLY-AWAY/RAPID DEPLOYMENT TEAMS

On June 6, 2002, the FBI created the fly-away/rapid deployment team unit to manage and support the field office-based rapid deployment teams and the newly created FBI Headquarters-based "fly squads." These specialized teams and squads lend counterterrorism knowledge and experience, language capabilities, and intelligence analysis support to FBI field offices and legal attachés whenever they are needed. Since September 11, 2001, the fly squads have been deployed on 38 occasions and have assisted in operations from Buffalo, New York, to the Gaza Strip.

EXPLOSIVE FORENSICS

To train for such events, the FBI's explosives unit commandeers junkyard cars and blows them up. The unit first must determine the type of explosive was used—that is, high or low explosives. Using cotton swabs, the unit will often recover the microscopic, unexploded trace evidence that yields the type of explosive used in the bomb. They look for unique characteristics of the explosive or chemical identifiers inserted into it by the manufacturer. In addition, the Special Agent laboratory examiners attempt to identify the components of the improvised explosive device. When successful, they feed the information back to the Special Agents working the case who will attempt to track the material back to the manufacturer and then to the individual who purchased the material and assembled the bomb.

This is all that remains of a truck bomb. The FBI must piece it back together in order to discover who was responsible for the bombing and what type of explosive was used.

In the case of the World Trade Center bombing, the agents were looking for one very important piece of evidence: the confidential vehicle identification number (CVIN). The CVIN is known only to the manufacturer and the FBI and is generally stamped on the vehicle's chassis in an obscure place; the exact position is known only to the manufacturer and the FBI.

FBI investigators sifting through the rubble in the parking garage found fragments from dozens of vehicles with vehicle identification numbers. After exhaustive research and interviewing hundreds of individuals, Special Agents discovered a number that corresponded to the number from a missing van that had been listed in the National Crime Information Center's (NCIC) computer. From the position and appearance of the pieces, they strongly suspect that the fragment came from the vehicle that carried the bomb.

This clue provided Special Agents with a trail back to the individual who rented the van and packed it with the explosives. Within a month, the crime scene search was complete, and the facts and evidence began to lead to the conclusion that it was the first attack by al Qaeda-trained terrorists in America. Four individuals were arrested by the FBI and later convicted in federal court of 38 crimes. Each terrorist received a sentence of 240 years in prison.

FINDING THE DNA OF TERRORIST BOMBS

According to the State Department, more than 85 percent of all terrorist attacks against U.S. citizens and interests during the past five years involved improvised explosive devices (IEDs), otherwise known as homemade bombs. Unlike manufactured military ordnance, these bombs often reflect the unique characteristics, or signatures, of the terrorist organizations or individuals who made them.

On the morning of July 28, 2004, a suicide bomber drove a car loaded with explosives into a crowd of job applicants standing outside a police station in Baqubah, Iraq. Sixty-eight people died, and 60 more were injured. Also on July 28, a bomb exploded in a Kabul mosque where Afghans were registering for upcoming elections. On July 30, three coordinated bombs exploded in Tashkent, Uzbekistan. On August 7, a bomb blew up in Baghdad near the Jordanian Embassy. FBI Special Agents, bomb technicians, forensic scientists, and ERT members were deployed to all these bombings.

On June 26, 1996, around 5,000 pounds of explosives packed into a truck exploded, drilling a crater 35 feet deep and ripping the front off an apartment building in the Khobar Towers complex at King Abdul Aziz Air Base near Dhahran, Saudi Arabia. That act of terrorism killed 19 Americans and injured scores of others, including Saudis and Bangladeshis. It was the deadliest bombing involving United States citizens in the Middle East since the October 23, 1983, truck bombings of a U.S. Marine Corps barracks in Beirut, Lebanon, which claimed 295 lives. The FBI deployed agents to investigate the Khobar Towers bombing.

These and other global terrorist bombings require a global response. The Terrorist Explosives Device Analytical Center (TEDAC), an FBI-led initiative, was created in December 2003 to provide a single federal program responsible for complete forensic and technical analysis, as well as timely distribution of intelligence regarding terrorist bombings collected by other entities and U.S. government partners worldwide.

For terrorists intent on destruction, bombs are easy and cheap to make, and horribly lethal. However, bombs are also unique and custom-made in a particular way, usually with an explosive charge, a fuse, and a trigger. "This means they leave clues," said one senior agent, "possibly DNA, fingerprints, identifiable trace evidence, but also a special 'signature' of design that can help us identify the bomb maker, and his [or her] organization." The FBI maximizes those clues and turns that information into intelligence that might prevent future attacks. Electronics specialists, explosives experts, engineers,

counterterrorism Special Agents, and analysts from the FBI, the Bureau of Alcohol, Firearms and Explosives, and other intelligence community agencies all contribute to TEDAC's intelligence efforts. The TEDAC team draws linkages between terrorist devices and their makers, who are sometimes continents away. They are looking for information that could keep the next bomb from going off. They also use the intelligence to develop new countermeasures and to train first responders on the IEDs that are actually being used by the terrorists.

"We have received many hundreds of devices, and the similarities uncovered in many of them suggest many terrorists are using the same set of bomb-making instructions," said one agent. "In the days ahead, the TEDAC will be expanding to increase the number of agencies directly involved; the number of devices, post-blast debris, and bomb-making materials it examines; and the amount of analysis TEDAC conducts on each device. But, our goal, however, is still to save lives."

SEPTEMBER 11

Eight years after the first World Trade Center bombing, al Qaeda terrorists struck again, and the attacks of September 11, 2001, marked a watershed in the history of the FBI. The attacks required an almost instantaneous change in the FBI's mission. Within minutes of the attacks, the FBI's headquarters command center, SIOC, provided analytical, logistical, and administrative support for the teams on the ground in New York, Pennsylvania, and at the Pentagon.

Flight attendants on the first plane that hit the World Trade Center's north tower had earlier begun calling in the seat assignments of some of the hijackers. Because SIOC existed and was online just minutes after the first airplane hit the north tower, the FBI began matching seat numbers to names on the flight manifest. Soon it knew the names of some of the hijackers, and it did not take long to link the attacks to Osama bin Ladin.

Lower Manhattan as seen from the harbor on September 11, 2001. Special Agent Leonard W. Hatton was the only active-duty Special Agent killed in the terrorist attack on the World Trade Center. Special Agent Hatton was on his way to work in the New York field office when he saw smoke and fire coming from the North Tower. On his own initiative, he responded directly to the World Trade Center site and, from the roof of the Marriott Hotel, he reported the second airliner strike to the south tower. To avoid falling debris, he moved from the roof and joined the New York fire department firefighters in evacuating occupants. SA Hatton was inside the WTC when the buildings collapsed. John O'Neil, who had run the counterterrorism unit at the New York field office before retiring from the FBI a month earlier, died in the attack while serving as head of security for the World Trade Center. *U.S. Coast Guard*

The highly polished black granite towers erected by the FBI Academy in Quantico, Virginia, serve as a memorial to September 11, 2001. The inscription on the side reads, "Dedicated to the courage, spirit, and sacrifice of those who perished in the struggle to save others, and those who persevered to protect freedom." Beneath the monument are artifacts from the World Trade Center, the site of the Pennsylvania crash, and the Pentagon.
Henry M. Holden

THE USA PATRIOT ACT

On October 26, 2001, President George W. Bush signed the USA Patriot Act. This anti-terrorism law provided the FBI with additional resources to hire new agents and critical support personnel, employ court approved wiretaps against potential terrorists more easily, share criminal investigative information with counterterrorism investigators, and more. The USA Patriot Act equips federal law enforcement officials with the tools they need to mount an effective, coordinated campaign against the terrorist enemies of the United States. It also revised counterproductive legal restraints that impaired law enforcement's ability to gather, analyze, and share critical terrorism-related intelligence information, as well as updated decades-old federal laws to account for the technological breakthroughs seen in recent years. For example, terrorists routinely use cell phones to plot their attacks; under the USA Patriot Act, law enforcement and intelligence officials are no longer hindered by statutes written in the era of rotary telephones. The act enhanced America's criminal laws against terrorism and, in some cases, increased the penalties for planning and participating in terrorist attacks and aiding terrorists. It also clarified that existing laws against terrorism apply to the new types of attacks planned by al Qaeda and other international terrorist organizations.

The FBI evidence response team meets outside the Pentagon hours after the September 11, 2001, attacks. *Department of Defense*

During the investigation of the 9/11 attacks on the World Trade Center, over 750 agents lived on the USS *Intrepid*, a decommissioned aircraft carrier that today serves as a museum on the west side of midtown Manhattan. The *Intrepid* is just a few miles from Ground Zero.
Henry M. Holden

A small portion of the fuselage from American Airlines Flight 11 that crashed into the World Trade Center tower is on display at the *Intrepid* Sea-Air-Space Museum. *Henry M. Holden*

There were 14 terrorist incidents and two preventions of terrorist attacks in the United States and its territories in 2001. Domestic terrorists carried out 12 of the 14 recorded incidents. One incident, the terrorist attacks of September 11, was perpetrated by international terrorists. Eight of the terrorist incidents that occurred in the United States in 2001 have been attributed to the Earth Liberation Front (ELF).

AA Flt.#11 Window/Fuselage Section

A new command center in New York City had to be established because the FBI field office was only a few blocks from Ground Zero. The FBI moved all the vehicles out of its block-long Hudson River pier garage on West 26th Street and set up a temporary command center. First fearing an airplane accident, evidence response teams from the New York office and the FBI's disaster squad were deployed to the site. "It was a day none of us will forget," said one agent. "We were standing not far from the north tower securing some of the airplane wreckage while bodies of people who had jumped to escape the flames fell around us. The roar of a low-flying plane caused us to look up. . . . When it knifed through the south tower, we all knew in that moment that America was under attack. We hoped it was only here, but it turned out to be worse than anything we had ever planned for."

"Our efforts, and those of other law enforcement and first responders, began as search-and-rescue missions at the sites," said another agent, "but, it was clear the crash sites were crime scenes, and the structured process of evidence collection began."

One hundred fifty-seven people died on the two planes that hit the towers, and a total of 3,024 people died in the combined attacks of September 11. The United States was at war against international terrorism.

Members of the FBI meet outside the Pentagon hours after terrorists flew American Airlines Fight 77 into the building on September 11, 2001.
Department of Defense

The site of the World Trade Center towers is shown as it looked three years after the attack. *Henry M. Holden*

Other teams of FBI Special Agents began a large-scale, worldwide terrorism investigation. The FBI quickly mobilized its employees to support the investigation—the largest, most complex, and comprehensive in its history. "Many of our personnel worked 16 or more hours a day for weeks," said one Special Agent. "We were all mad as hell, and we were going to do whatever it took."

Several hundred Special Agents traveled around the world to interview detained terrorist suspects in the Sudan—where Bin Laden had lived—and other locations. FBI personnel worked around the clock, chasing down thousands of leads and conducting thousands of interviews. Others searched through mountains of debris at Ground Zero, the Fresh Kills Landfill on Staten Island (where the World Trade Center wreckage had been brought), the Pentagon, and in the field of Stony Creek Township, Pennsylvania, the site of the United Airlines Flight 93 crash. They were searching for clues, identifying remains, and examining and categorizing tons of evidence.

Following the terrorist attacks on the World Trade Center and the Pentagon, the FBI assigned over 7,000 Special Agents, over 250 laboratory and other personnel, and 20 legats overseas to pursue leads and coordinate the investigation with their foreign counterparts.

The FBI's Terrorist Research and Analytical Center uses the Terrorist Information System (TIS) online database to support the Bureau's counterterrorism program. The TIS has over 300,000 individuals and 3,000 organizations in the database. The center analyzes information and uses it to generate forecasts of potential threats.

On December 21, 1988, Pan American Airways Flight 103 exploded, killing 249 people. Pieces of the plane fell onto the Scottish town of Lockerbie, killing 11 people on the ground. The aircraft was destroyed by a bomb built into a Toshiba radio cassette player. In cooperation with Scottish authorities, the FBI played an indispensable role in attaining the murder conviction of a Libyan national for the bombing.

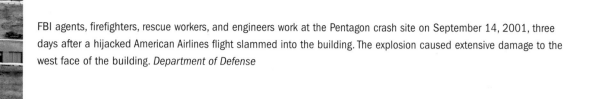

FBI agents, firefighters, rescue workers, and engineers work at the Pentagon crash site on September 14, 2001, three days after a hijacked American Airlines flight slammed into the building. The explosion caused extensive damage to the west face of the building. *Department of Defense*

Two days after the attack on the Pentagon, the west face of the building shows the gaping gash where almost 200 people died. The FBI had agents working 100 hours a week during this crisis. The terrorist attacks of September 11, 2001, marked a dramatic escalation in a trend toward more destructive terrorist attacks that began in the 1980s. The attacks of September 11 produced casualty figures greater than Pearl Harbor and more than ten times higher than those of the 1983 marine corps barracks attack in Beirut, Lebanon. *Department of Defense*

FBI investigators found letters handwritten in Arabic in three separate locations. The first was in a suitcase of hijacker Mohamed Atta, which did not make his connecting flight, American Airlines Flight 11. The second was in a vehicle parked at Dulles International Airport belonging to hijacker Nawaf Alhazmi. The third was at the crash site in Pennsylvania. The letters indicated the terrorists had declared war on the United States and that the hijackers had an alarming willingness to die.

The voice and flight data recorders from United Airlines Flight 93, which crashed in Pennsylvania, confirmed that the passengers engaged in a fight for their lives with their four hijackers, saving the lives of perhaps hundreds of people on the ground in Washington, D.C. The FBI evidence response team later found a burned fragment of a passport identifying one of the hijackers. Within days after the 9/11 terrorists attacks, the FBI identified the 19 hijackers using flight, credit card, bank, and other records.

After the attacks, the FBI has at least 150 ongoing investigations into al Qaeda activities in the United States alone. This is where training pays off. Most of the leads will not pan out, but as one agent put it, "We have to follow up on every single lead. We can't afford not to."

Today the FBI's overriding mission is to prevent acts of terrorism before they happen. Each Special Agent undergoes a minimum of 40 hours of counterterrorism training, which is managed by the counterterrorism division at FBI Headquarters and carried out in Quantico, every field office, resident agency, and legat.

TERRORIST FINANCING OPERATIONS

Terrorists, their networks, and their support structures require funding in some form in order to exist and operate. Whether the funding and financial support is minimal or substantial, it leaves a financial trail that can be traced, tracked, and exploited for pro-active and reactive purposes. Being able to track financial transactions and links after a terrorist act has occurred or terrorist activity has been identified represents only a small portion of the mission, though. The key lies in exploiting financial information in efforts to identify previously unknown or "sleeper" terrorist cells, recognize potential terrorist activity and planning, and prevent potential terrorist acts. The FBI bolstered its ability to effectively combat terrorism through the formation of the terrorist financing operations section (TFOS).

The TFOS mission includes: conducting financial analysis of terrorist suspects and their financial support structures worldwide; coordinating joint participation, liaison, and outreach efforts to utilize financial resources of private, government, and foreign entities; working jointly with the intelligence community to further terrorist investigations and to aid identification of sleeper terrorist suspects; and providing the financial component to FBI classified counterterrorism investigations.

Narco-terrorism is fueled by drug money and is used to fund political assassinations and long-term terror and unrest in a country. This plane-load of drugs was intercepted before its deadly cargo could be sold to Americans. *Henry M. Holden collection*

COUNTERTERRORISM CASE: AHMED RESSAM

On December 14, 1999, Ahmed Ressam, a 32-year-old Algerian, was arrested at Port Angeles, Washington, while attempting to enter the United States with components used to manufacture improvised explosive devices (IEDs).

He later admitted that he planned to bomb Los Angeles International Airport on the eve of the millennium 2000 celebrations. Forensic scientists from both the Royal Canadian Mounted Police (RCMP) and the FBI examined the evidence in this case. An FBI laboratory explosives unit examiner compared evidence found in Ressam's motel room in Vancouver with items seized in Port Angeles.

The RCMP laboratory identified the presence of explosives and developed a DNA profile from a pair of pants and shoes recovered in Ressam's apartment in Montreal. Lab technicians found several holes in the pants that were consistent with an acid spill. With this information, the FBI Seattle field office examined Ressam's legs and discovered a large burn. At the trial, a doctor specializing in burns testified that the burn on Ressam's leg was consistent with an acid burn.

In the FBI laboratory, agents discovered a piece of hair on a piece of clear tape inside one of the four time-delay fusing systems. The trace evidence unit examined the hair and determined it had the same microscopic characteristics as Ressam's hair.

Latent prints developed on the four timing devices, and a map of Los Angeles showing three airports circled were associated with Ressam. Thirteen of Ressam's fingerprints were found on a date book, which included the addresses of two of Bin Laden collaborators. It also contained the addresses of the firms that Ressam used to obtain the electronic components and precursor chemicals for the manufacturing of the explosives.

In addition, investigators found that Ressam had made credit card purchases at several electronics shops in Montreal, Canada. An explosives unit examiner traveled to Canada and purchased the same items, in order to demonstrate to the jury that Ressam could have purchased electronic components that were consistent with the ones used in the construction of the time-delay fusing systems recovered in the trunk of the rental vehicle.

After reviewing the items recovered in Montreal and Vancouver, the explosives unit examiner obtained several rolls of tape and a small piece of wire insulation for comparison. Later, a forensic chemist determined that the packaging tape and clear tape recovered in Ressam's Montreal apartment were consistent in physical characteristics and chemical composition to those removed from the time-delay fusing systems. The FBI determined that the pieces of tape removed from them could have originated from the roll of packaging tape and clear tape recovered from Ressam's apartment. In addition, a small piece of wire insulation was recovered from the Vancouver motel room. The FBI chemist determined that it was consistent in physical characteristics and chemical composition to the wires used in the time-delay fusing systems. Ahmed Ressam was later convicted in federal court of conspiring to commit an act of international terrorism and eight related charges.

Financial terrorism is a simple concept; it is the monetary support of terrorist acts or of those who encourage, plan, or engage in terrorism. "We investigate the 'who, what, where, when and how' and try to identify terrorists and terrorist cells by following their money trails to stop their plans before the bomb goes off," said the chief of the TFOS.

"The FBI and its training is constantly evolving," said one SAC. "The crimes we are fighting cross international boundaries. Terrorism we know is often funded by other crimes. Our agents now have to be investigators and intelligence officers," he continued. "A Special Agent working a healthcare fraud case has to track the money. She [or he] now has to think, 'Is it going to a terrorist group?'"

"The money street gang drug dealers bring in eventually finds its way back to a terrorist group in South America," said one senior agent. For example, most of Bin Laden's money comes from heroin traffic. "In some way the crimes are all connected," continued the senior agent. "If we get enough information, our agents can connect the dots."

As the events of September 11, 2001, demonstrated, the terrorist threats facing the United States are formidable. Between 1991 and 2001, 74 terrorist incidents were recorded in the United States. During this same period, an additional 62 terrorist plots within the United States were prevented by United States law enforcement. For every successful terrorist attack mounted in the United States, nearly 20 anti-United States attacks are carried out around the world. Between 1996 and 2001, these overseas attacks killed 75 Americans and wounded an additional 606.

On October 12, 2000, suicide terrorists attacked the U.S. Navy destroyer USS *Cole* by steering a small boat alongside the ship as it was refueling in the Yemeni port of Aden. The boat exploded, tearing a hole 40 feet wide at the waterline of the *Cole* and killing 17 United States sailors. The FBI deployed over 100 Special Agents from the counterterrorism division, the FBI laboratory, and various field offices to Aden. Investigators found human teeth in the hull of the *Cole* that led to the identification of the al Qaeda cell and others involved in the conspiracy to carry out the bombing.

FBI photographers took pictures of the crime scene that assisted in identifying the remains of the victims and provided detailed photographic information regarding the impact of the explosion. Later, FBI personnel from the explosives unit, investigative support section, and special photographic unit, as well as bomb technicians and agents from the New York, and Jackson, Mississippi, field offices traveled to Ingalls Shipbuilding in Pascagoula, Mississippi—where the damaged *Cole* had been brought—to examine the ship for additional evidence.

FBI SWAT teams are well trained and equipped to execute dangerous raids (including drug raids), high-risk search and arrest warrants, and barricade situations. The equipment and weapons of the SWAT and HRT are different from the usual weapons of the law enforcement officers on the street. The hostage rescue teams (HRTs) use long-range, high-caliber rifles. Even their uniform is selected to provide camouflage and create psychological fear when an assault takes place. The operators are wearing Darth Vader-like masks, black shirts, black fatigue pants, and heavy black boots. The uniform is meant to, and does, intimidate those bent on doing harm.

One of the functions of the TFOS is to develop predictive models and conduct data analysis that will lead to the identification of sleeper terrorist cells and suspects. "We have spent the past three years transforming operations and realigning resources to meet the threats of the post-September 11 environment," said one senior agent.

Money laundering is a major contributing factor of terrorism. Launderers attempt, often with success, to send illicit proceeds through legal channels—front companies or bogus charities—in such a way as to conceal their source and ultimate use, which sometimes is for the support of terrorism. Since 9/11 the FBI has seized more than $135 million in terrorist-related assets and has stopped more than 300 individuals and entities (mostly bogus charities) from funding or having ties with terrorist groups. Being able to identify and track these financial trails after a terrorist act has occurred is important, but the challenge for the Special Agent is to achieve the mission of prevention by exploiting the financial information to identify sleeper or undetected terrorists and/or terrorist cells.

COUNTERINTELLIGENCE

As the lead counterintelligence (CI) agency in the United States, the FBI is responsible for identifying and neutralizing ongoing national security threats. The counterintelligence division provides centralized management and oversight for all foreign counterintelligence (FCI) investigations.

It ensures that offensive operations and investigations are fully coordinated with the U.S. intelligence community and focused on those countries, foreign powers, or entities that pose the most significant threats to the United States.

"We are charged with investigating just about anything we have that is worth stealing," said one senior agent. "It can range from pharmaceutical and technological secrets to military and telecommunications secrets." Specially trained Special Agents and counterintelligence experts monitor and neutralize foreign intelligence operations. They investigate violations of federal espionage laws, misuse of classified data, and other criminal matters related to national security.

"It's a big job, and our agents need patience and tenacity," said another senior agent. "Some investigations take years. Once we have identified a threat, we may have to infiltrate the organization first, and then develop a case. Sometimes we may not make an arrest or pursue a criminal prosecution. We think strategically before making arrests, sometimes opting to delay a suspect's arrest to allow more opportunity for surveillance that might disclose other conspirators or other criminal plans. We have used this approach to great effect in organized crime cases and espionage investigations, and members of our safe-streets task forces use it in their fight against street gangs," he continued. "It is sometimes better to feed misinformation. In other cases, we may deport the non-U.S. citizens and arrest the U.S. citizens involved in the crime."

The FBI's counterintelligence program is involved in international terrorism threats, weapons of mass destruction threats, and attacks on the nation's critical infrastructures. "We feel the threats from countries which consider the United States their primary intelligence target, adversary, or threat will likely increase," he said. "The most desirable U.S. targets will be political and military plans, technology, and economic institutions in both the government and private sectors.

"We are seeing foreign intelligence activities increasingly characterized by the use of sophisticated and secure communication technology to handle recruited agents, and since these threats are asymmetrical, they are more likely to occur almost anywhere in the United States."

THE FOREIGN COUNTERINTELLIGENCE PROGRAM

The FBI is responsible for detecting and counteracting foreign intelligence activity that gathers information that adversely affects United States national interests or security. It conducts foreign counterintelligence investigations under the authority of Executive Order 12333 and acts of Congress. The investigative priorities of the foreign counterintelligence (FCI) program are to:

· Prevent or neutralize the foreign acquisition of weapons of mass destruction (WMD) technology or equipment;

· Prevent the penetration of the United States intelligence community;

· Prevent the penetration of United States government agencies or contractors

· Prevent the compromise of United States critical national assets

· Conduct aggressive counterintelligence (CI) operations focusing on those countries that constitute the most significant threat to United States strategic interests.

The FBI is engaged in an ongoing CI effort that involves protecting trade secrets and guarding against operations or disinformation campaigns that would disadvantage the United States. "It strikes at the heart of our national security; our political, military, and economic strengths; our position in the world; and our future as a country," said the senior agent. "That's why only terrorism, with its threat of direct attacks and bombings and mass casualties, ranks above it. In the Cold War, the threat was symmetrical. It was predictable, clear, and geographically limited to the Soviet Union and the bloc countries. Today, the threat is asymmetrical, and it is coming at us from all directions." He continued, "Intelligence itself—how it's collected, what's collected, how it's managed and analyzed—is just as crucial to the success of counterintelligence as it is to the success of counterterrorism."

Given these new threat scenarios, the FBI has made significant changes in the analysis model. "Our strategic analysis unit is dedicated to connecting the dots," the senior agent explained. "Rather than aggregating what has already been reported, these analysts posit hypotheses regarding threats, and then compile evidence to prove or disprove these hypotheses. Our aim is to make our analysts actively inquire of data rather than have them be passive recipients of data.

"For years, embassies and consulates were a basis of operations for intelligence services. Now foreign governments are also using students, visiting delegations, scientists, and false front companies to get at our secrets. And the threat is just as severe in places like Alabama, Kentucky, Maine, and Iowa, as it is in New York or Washington [D.C.], because the classified projects, the universities, and the corporations being targeted exist throughout the U.S."

An FBI Special Agent SWAT/hostage negotiator at an August 2004 exercise called Amalgam Virgo '04 held at Portland International Airport in Oregon. It involved a simulated hijacking of a plane with weapons of mass destruction threats.

At the request of the International Criminal Tribunal for the former Yugoslavia (ICTY), a team of 62 FBI Special Agents, crime scene investigators, and others made several trips to Kosovo in 1999 to recover human remains from mass graves.

The FBI's mission in Kosovo encompassed the examination of the victims through field autopsies and crime scene work conducted by the FBI laboratory and evidence response team (ERT) specialists. The results of the FBI team's evidence gathering and forensic examinations were turned over to the International Criminal Tribunal for the former Yugoslavia (ICTY) upon completion of the assignment.

Once the body is exhumed, an attempt to identify it is made. In the case of the ethnic cleansing in Kosovo, thousands were never identified.

"Legats" are senior FBI Special Agents stationed at 54 offices around the world. Their role was created during World War II as the FBI's special foreign intelligence branch and they were assigned to Latin and South America. Today, legats' goals are to stop foreign crime and keep it as far from American shores as possible, and to help solve international crimes as soon as possible. They generally do not carry firearms in their host country and must develop a rapport with the local law enforcement if they are to be effective. Their purpose is strictly coordination; they do not conduct foreign intelligence gathering or counterintelligence investigations. The rules for information sharing are generally spelled out in a formal agreement between the United States and the legats' host countries.

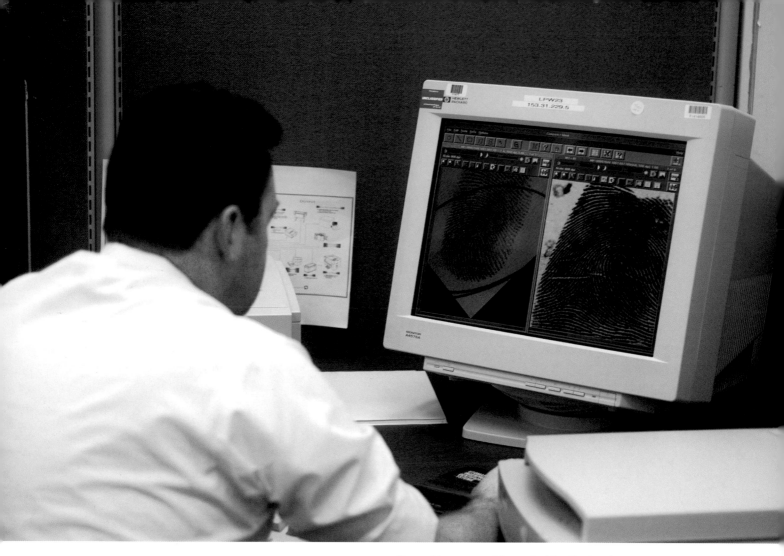

The rapid response of fingerprint identification through the Integrated Automated Fingerprint Identification System (IAFIS) makes it possible to identify fugitives while they are still in police custody. Fingerprints can be recorded on a standard fingerprint card or recorded digitally and transmitted electronically to the FBI for comparison. By comparing fingerprints at the scene of a crime with the fingerprint record of suspected persons, officials can establish absolute proof of the presence or identity of a person.

TERRORIST SCREENING CENTER

From December 1, 2003, to March 23, 2004, the FBI's Terrorist Screening Center (TSC) received 2,045 calls from national law enforcement personnel. These calls were based on potential matches with known or suspected terrorists and resulted in 835 positive identifications. Some had been apprehended on various charges, while others had been developed into informants or subjected to surveillance. One example: A local police department contacted the TSC following an NCIC "hit" after an arrest on a minor charge. TSC contacted the local JTTF, who interviewed the subject regarding his involvement with a domestic terrorist group. The subject agreed to cooperate with the FBI and is now an informant on domestic terrorism matters.

Presidential decision directive (PDD) 39 extended FBI investigative authority beyond United States borders when United States interests are harmed or threatened. Since 1984, the FBI has carried out over 300 extraterritorial investigations, including the September 11 attacks and the bombings of Khobar Towers in Saudi Arabia, two United States embassies in East Africa, and the USS *Cole* in the Yemenese port of Aden.

The FBI assumed crime scene jurisdiction at the Pentagon terrorist attack site on September 21, 2001, from the Arlington County Fire Department in Virginia. Arthur Eberhart, Special Agent in Charge of the FBI crime scene investigation at the Pentagon, turned over control of the site to U.S. Army Major General James T. Jackson's command and the Military District of Washington in a transfer ceremony on September 26, 2001. Here, Major General Jackson presents Eberhart with a poster-sized photo of the American flag being unfurled from the roof of the Pentagon on September 12, 2001, the day after terrorists crashed a hijacked jetliner into the building. The flag was a commemorative gift to FBI crime scene investigators, who continued their operations in a nearby parking lot.

Although various executive orders, presidential decision directives (PDD), and congressional statutes address the issue of terrorism, there is no single federal law specifically making terrorism a crime. Terrorists are arrested and convicted under existing criminal statutes.

Critical to counterterrorism efforts is the use of biometric and biographical information—such as fingerprints, DNA, photographs, and biographical information from foreign sources—to establish a person's identity conclusively. The FBI's criminal justice information services (CJIS) division has led several overseas deployments to gather and exchange fingerprints of known and suspected terrorists. CJIS has obtained fingerprints and other identifying information for more than 10,000 terrorist suspects and detainees from more than 16 countries. The Department of Defense and the CJIS are adding selected enemy combatant fingerprints to existing fingerprint databases and making them available for military, law enforcement, and homeland security needs. CJIS is also working with the Department of Defense, the navy, army, and marine corps to provide identification services and assistance in Iraq and Afghanistan.

The United States Postal Inspection Service,
Federal Bureau of Investigation and
U.S. DOT Office of Inspector General

$120,000REWARD

A reward is being offered of up to $120,000 for information leading to the arrest and conviction of the individual(s) responsible for the mailing of letters containing the poison ricin and ricin derivative.

Threatening communications inside each envelope made reference to pending hours-of-service regulations by the Department of Transportation; specifically, the number of hours truck drivers would be allowed to drive before a required rest period. The substance in the first letter was enclosed in a small metal vial.

"caution RICIN POISON"
"Enclosed in sealed container"
"Do not open without proper protection"

First letter discovered in Greenville, SC on 10/15/2003:

The following is a representation of the language contained in the threat letter:

"to the department of transportation: I'm a fleet owner of a tankard company.
I have easy access to castor pulp. If my demand is dismissed I'm capable of making Ricin.
My demand is simple, January 4 2004 starts the new hours of service for trucks which include a ridiculous ten hours in the sleeper berth. Keep at eight.
You have been warned this is the only letter that will be sent by me."

Second letter postmarked in Chattanooga, TN on 10/17/2003:

"Department of Transportation

If you change the hours of service on January 4, 2004 I will turn D.C. into a ghost town
The powder on the letter is RICIN
have a nice day"

        Fallen Angel

The person(s) responsible for these threats infers a connection to the trucking/transportation industry, but any potential leads should be reported.

Anyone having information, contact the Tip Line 1-866-839-6241

All information will be held in strict confidence. Reward payment will be made in accordance with conditions of Postal Service Reward Poster 296, dated February 2000.

All Information will be Kept Confidential!

Domestic terrorism is now a constant concern. In October 2004, the FBI, U.S. Postal Inspection Service, U.S. Department of Transportation, and Office of Inspector General increased the reward money to $120,000 for information leading to the arrest and conviction of the individual(s) responsible for sending threatening letters containing ricin into postal facilities in Greenville, South Carolina, and Chattanooga, Tennessee, in October 2003.

CONCLUSION

Today, terrorism is the most significant threat to the national security of the United States. Foreign state sponsors of international terrorism, formalized terrorist groups, and loosely affiliated radical terrorists now target the entire population of the United States. Over the next five years, the FBI believes the number of international state-sponsored terrorist organizations will decline. However, "Al Qaeda and its affiliates will remain the most significant threat over the next five years," said one senior agent. Privately sponsored terrorist groups will increasingly cooperate with one another to achieve their ends. These alliances will be short and will challenge the FBI to identify specific threats.

The September 11, 2001, attacks woke us up to the deadly threat of modern terrorism and the need for bold action. While there is still work to be done, the FBI has made significant progress with reforming its efforts. The FBI's counterterrorism program has made comprehensive changes in order to meet its primary mission of preventing terrorist operations before they occur. Its agents' efforts to protect America's critical national assets such as advanced technologies, weapons systems, military capacities, and classified information have gone largely unreported—yet they do not waiver. An individual who planned to set off a radioactive "dirty bomb" was apprehended. The FBI also identified a farm in Oregon as a terrorist training camp. In northern Virginia, the FBI took down the Virginia Jihad Network, which was using a site for paintball games to train for martyrdom operations. Two leaders of a mosque were arrested for allegedly plotting to buy a shoulder-fired missile. The intelligence for this came from Iraq. In March 2004, another individual was indicted in Virginia federal court for possession of illegal firearms, grenades, chemicals, explosive powder, and weaponized ricin.

While the CT division at FBI Headquarters manages the effort, it is carried out by every field office, resident agency, and legat. Headquarters collects and computerizes all field data on suspected terrorists groups and their activities that pose a potential threat to the United States. With these efforts, largely achieved through the hard work and diligence of FBI Special Agents and with the support of the American people, the FBI is confident that the United States will prevail in the war against terrorism.

PREVENTING TERRORIST ATTACKS

Surveillance: Are you aware of anyone video recording or monitoring activities, taking notes, or using cameras, maps, binoculars, etc., near key facilities or events?

Suspicious questioning: Are you aware of anyone attempting to gain information in person, by phone, mail, e-mail, etc., regarding a key facility or people who work there?

Tests of security: Are you aware of any attempts to penetrate or test physical security or procedures at a key facility or event?

Acquiring supplies: Are you aware of anyone attempting to improperly acquire explosives, weapons, ammunition, dangerous chemicals, uniforms, badges, flight manuals, access cards, or identification documents for a key facility or event, or to legally obtain items under suspicious circumstances that could be used in a terrorist attack?

Suspicious persons: Are you aware of anyone who does not appear to belong in the workplace, neighborhood, business establishment, or near a key facility or event?

Dry runs: Have you observed any behavior that appears to be preparation for a terrorist act, such as mapping out routes, playing out scenarios with other people, monitoring key facilities or events, timing traffic lights or traffic flow, or other suspicious activities?

Deploying assets: Have you observed abandoned vehicles, stockpiling of suspicious materials, or persons being deployed near a key facility or event? If you answered yes to any of the above, or have observed any suspicious activity that may relate to terrorism, contact the joint terrorist task force or the law enforcement counterterrorism agency closest to you immediately. Your tip could save the lives of innocent people.

Appendix A

FBI HALL OF HONOR

The FBI honors its Special Agents killed in the line of duty as the result of a direct adversarial force or at the hand of an adversary. The names of these agents, who are appropriately termed "service martyrs," are included on a permanent plaque so that their ultimate sacrifice will always be remembered. The inscription on this service martyr plaque reads: "In memory of Special Agents of the Federal Bureau of Investigation who were killed in the line of duty as the direct result of an adversarial action." Thirty-four Special Agents were designated as service martyrs as of September 2001.

Service Martyrs' Wall

The FBI also honors those agents who lose their lives in the performance of their duty, but not necessarily during an adversarial confrontation (signified below by *). This includes situations involving "hot pursuit" of criminals and when death results from the agent taking immediate action to save one or more lives. A separate plaque memorializing the sacrifice of these agents reads: "In memory of Special Agents of the Federal Bureau of Investigation who lost their lives in the performance of a law enforcement duty." Fourteen Special Agents have been honored for giving their lives in the performance of their law enforcement duties.

SPECIAL AGENTS—DIED IN SERVICE

Edwin C. Shanahan	1925	Ronald A. Williams	1975
Paul E. Reynolds	1929	Trenwith S. Basford	*1977
Albert L. Ingle	*1931	Mark A. Kirkland	*1977
Raymond J. Caffrey	1933	Johnnie L. Oliver	1979
W. Carter Baum	1934	Charles W. Elmore	1979
Herman E. Hollis	1934	J. Robert Porter	1979
Samuel P. Crowley	1934	Terry Burnett Hereford	*1982
Nelson B. Klein	1935	Robert W. Conners	*1982
Wimberly W. Baker	1937	Charles L. Ellington	*1982
Truette E. Rowe	1937	Michael James Lynch	*1982
William R. Ramsey	1938	Robin L. Aherns	1985
Hubert J. Treacy, Jr.	1942	Jerry Dove	1986
Percy E. Foxworth	*1943	Benjamin P. Grogan	1986
Harold Dennis Haberfeld	*1943	James K. McAllister	*1986
Richard Blackstone Brown	*1943	Scott K. Carey	*1988
Joseph J. Brock	1952	L. Douglas Abram	1990
J. Brady Murphy	1953	John L. Bailey	1990
Richard P. Horan	1957	Stanley Ronquist, Jr.	*1992
Terry R. Anderson	1966	Martha Dixon Martinez	1994
Douglass M. Price	1968	Michael John Miller	1994
Anthony Palmisano	1969	William H. Christian, Jr.	1995
Edwin R. Woodriffe	1969	Charles Leo Reed	1996
Gregory W. Spinelli	1973	Paul A. Leveille	*1999
Jack R. Coler	1975	Leonard W. Hatton	2001

Appendix B

ACRONYMS AND DEFINITIONS

Acronyms:
ADCI—assistant director, counterintelligence
ADIC—assistant director in charge
AFIT—advanced firearms instructional techniques
ASAC—assistant special agent in charge
AUSA—assistant U.S. attorney (general)
BOI—Bureau of Investigation
CAT— crisis action teams
CDC—center for disease control
CITAC—Computer Investigation Threat Assessment Center
CIRG—critical incident response group
CNU—crisis negotiation unit
CODIS—Combined DNA Index System
CQB—close-quarters battle
CT—counterterrorism
CVIN—confidential vehicle identification number
DNA—deoxyribonucleic acid
DODPI—Department of Defense Polygraph Institute
DOJ—Department of Justice
DT—defensive tactics
ERT—evidence response team
ETI—enterprise theory of investigation
FBIHQ—FBI Headquarters
FATS—firearms training simulation
FOIA—Freedom of Information Act
FTO—foreign terrorist organization
G-man—"government man"
HMRU—hazard materials response unit
HRT—hostage rescue team
IAFIS—Integrated Automated Fingerprint Identification System
ICE—Immigration and Customs Enforcement
ICTU—investigative computer training unit
IED—improvised explosive devices
JTTF—joint terrorism task force
LE—law enforcement
legat—legal attaché
NAT—new agent trainee
NARB—New Agent Review Board
NCIC—National Crime Information Center
NICS—National Instant Criminal Background Check System
NJTTF—national joint terrorism task force

NOTS—new operator training school
NTSB—National Transportation Safety Board
OJT—On-the-job training
OPR—Office of Professional Responsibility
PRT—physical fitness test
PDD—presidential decision directive
PSI—personnel security interview
PT—physical test
RA—resident agencies
RICO —Racketeer Influenced and Corrupt Organization statute
SAC—special agent in charge
SAQQ—special agent qualifications questionnaire
SCI— sensitive compartmentalized information
SIOC—Strategic Information and Operations Center
SWAT—special weapons and tactics
TDY—temporary duty
TEDAC—Terrorist Explosives Device Analytical Center
TEVOC—tactical emergency vehicle operators course
TFOS—terrorist financing operations section
TIS—Terrorist Information System
TSC—Terrorist Screening Center
UC—undercover
WMD—weapons of mass destruction

Definitions:
Acrophobia—fear of heights
Fidelity—loyalty, faithfulness
Frangible bullets—lead-free bullets that are 100 percent safe when hitting anything as hard as or harder than the bullet. A frangible bullet turns to dust when it hits something hard, and it shoots just as well as plated bullets.
Indictment—a formal accusation of wrongdoing, usually issued by a grand jury. An individual charged by indictment is presumed innocent until proven guilty at some later criminal proceedings.
Integrity—honesty and uprightness
Money laundering—the process by which proceeds from a criminal activity are disguised to conceal their illicit origins
On the job—generic expression for an active-duty law enforcement officer.
Posse Comitatus—a force of able-bodied private citizens summoned to assist in maintaining public order.

Racketeer Influenced and Corrupt Organization (RICO) Statute—a federal statute designed to combat the infiltration of racketeers and organized crime into legal organizations engaged in interstate commerce. The statute also applies to individuals, businesses, political protest groups, and terrorist organizations.

Release the crime scene—allow it to be opened for cleanup or to public access

Squad—a team of Special Agents dedicated to one enforcement discipline (i.e. cyber crime)

Statute of limitations—a time limit during which a crime can be prosecuted. In the United States only three crimes are unbound by any statute of limitation: homicide, tax evasion, and espionage.

Stove piping—the vertical integration of an organization where there is no cross communication

Street agent—an agent removed from the policy and administrative decision-making processes

Walk-in—a volunteer who walks into an embassy or consulate and offers his or her services as a spy

Index

To Be a U.S. Air Force Pilot
ISBN 0-7603-1791-7

U.S. Counter-Terrorist Forces
ISBN 0-7603-1363-6

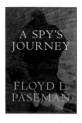

A Spy's Journey: A CIA Memoir
ISBN 0-7603-2066-7

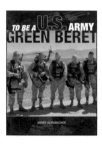

To Be a U.S. Army Green Beret
ISBN 0-7603-2107-8

To Be a U.S. Army Ranger
ISBN 0-7603-1314-8

To Be a U.S. Navy SEAL
ISBN 0-7603-1404-7

To Be a U.S. Marine
ISBN 0-7603-1788-7

Bomb Squads
ISBN 0-7603-0560-9

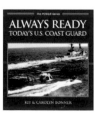

**Always Ready:
Today's U.S. Coast Guard**
ISBN 0-7603-1727-5